P9-DDY-884

The Church Alive

By Samuel M. Shoemaker

HOW YOU CAN HELP OTHER PEOPLE

HOW YOU CAN FIND HAPPINESS

THE CHURCH ALIVE

THE CHURCH ALIVE

BY

Samuel M. Shoemaker,

D.D., S.T.D.

Rector of Calvary Church In New York

E. P. Dutton & Co., Inc.

New York 1950

FIRST EDITION

To
My People of Calvary Church
amongst whom I have learned most of what has
been written in this book,
with affection and gratitude;
and to
Dick and Ken and Jack and Dave and Bob and Brews and Fred and Rudy and Bud and John and Jaap and Don and Kelly and Jim and Roger and Ray and George and Bill and Ed and Scott and Johann and Neale and Bardee and Charlie and Al and Arnold and Crawford and Peter—and many others,—with high hopes and sheer envy at the years of ministry
that lie before them.

CONTENTS

The Church Alive

Introduction

HOWEVER manifold and complex the facts of our time may be, it is not hard to fit them into some kind of pattern, if only you begin with the Christian point of view. The world is still in God's hands and operating according to His laws. He deals with us by love if possible, and He deals with us by judgment if necessary. This seems to be a time when the prideful sin of man has gone so far, and created such consequences, that God is speaking to us principally in judgment, and the earth is in turmoil. Yet we have a profound and uplifting word of wisdom and promise in Isaiah (26:9) who says, "When thy judgments are in the earth, the inhabitants of the world will learn righteousness." At least they will learn what happens when you do not have righteousness, and this gives them pause—the pause that may be prelude to penitence.

Our day is seeing an intensified expression of the struggle between Good and Evil which has gone on since Eden. There has always been warfare between those who believe in God and seek to order their lives and their world by taking Him into account, and those who do not believe in Him and let their lives and their world drift with nothing to order them but human wisdom. Today the anti-God forces find leadership, company, a world view and a world strategy in Communism. The pro-God forces center in the Christian Church. Upon which of these two forces wins out in our time depends the nature of the world for centuries to come. The Church does not have at its command the kind of resources which Communism can muster; its power is mostly of a spiritual nature, and has effect in changed human personalities and changed human relations. Sometimes its methods seem very inadequate and slow in a day when human forces move swiftly; and very often its world view is inadequate. Yet, with all its human imperfections, the Church and the things for which it stands hold the key to any future which seems to be worth living on this planet.

This means that the Church is the most important institution on earth. It is important, not only because the spiritual life of man comes first and determines the nature of the rest of his life, and not only because it helps man to live as he should in the amazing adventure of crossing this planet, but also because, in the long run, it will be found that Christianity alone is on the side of man—and the cause of Christianity is largely in the hands of the Church. Christianity's insistent contention with man about his sins is one proof that Christianity is his friend; and this must be seen in the light of Christianity's abiding concern about man in his predicament. The Church, whatever the faults of the human beings within it, is the custodian of this message of God's love and the revelation of Himself in Christ: this cannot be fully accepted and entered into by man outside the fellowship of the Church. Therefore the leaders of the Church are probably more important today than any other group of men on earth. They ought to be ceaselessly in our prayers, from the Pope to the most obscure leader of a Quaker meeting. The little man in the black coat, the rector who seems to make little dent in the community, the "father" who is so busy with his round of services–it is easy to play them down, and think them a race apart, and consider their task of reforming human nature a stab at the impossible; but they hold in their hands the one force that can redeem and renew our world. Upon the goodness, devotion and effectiveness of men like them depends, far more than we think, the sweetness and sanity and even the survival of the world.

I meet and talk with a great many ministers. I like parsons. They are ordinary men, like myself, trying to do an extraordinary job. They want to be more effective, as I do. This book has been written, not as a *magnum opus* on the ministry, but to try to bring them some help, drawn from my own and others' experience. I have written it with three groups of clergy (or near-clergy) in mind:

(1) Theological students who need some orientation to the work they will soon be doing, even while their main occupation now is preparatory, and who often get lost in a maze of ecclesiastical information which does not come together and make sense for them *now;*

(2) Young men already in the ministry who are not striking fire, who may not have found themselves spiritually, yet whose minds are crystallizing every day and hardening into patterns, and who desperately want to exercise a "spiritual ministry" and are searching for ways to discover what that means;

(3) Older men in the ministry who have lost the flame they once knew, feel lonely and discouraged, and have about settled down to mediocrity and spiritual ineffectiveness.

In addition to these three groups, I hope that the book may also have something to say to two groups of laymen as well: (1) the young layman who is searching for the best place to invest his life, and is ready to consider the claims upon him of the Christian ministry, and wants to know something of what the ministry means; and (2) the layman whose call is to take his faith with him into his office, his plant, his studio, his school, and who wants spiritual help in practicing this most important lay-ministry.

Let me say a further word here to men in seminaries, and to men already ordained.

Thoreau once said of students, "I mean that they should not play life, or *study* it merely, while the community supports them at this expensive game, but earnestly *live* it from end to end." If a man has been truly converted before he gets to seminary, it probably will not "throw" him; but if, like many men when they go to seminary, he is seeking his own salvation as well as that of others in the future, I feel for him. There is so much learning apart from doing, so much theory, so much delay, so much vicarious living in the future which is a kind of unreality, so much knowledge and so little supernatural life, that many a man who comes in warm is soon cooled off, and some never regain the enthusiasm which they felt in their first dedication to the ministry. There is, of course, something very immature in the man who wants to be "up-and-at-'em" the minute he decides to be a minister; he needs a great deal of information, of exposure, of settling in, which he has not yet had. But why should this kill the flame out of men's spirits, as so often it does? Jesus said that John the Baptist was "a *burning* and a *shining* light." Can we not have the warmth, as well as the illumination?

It may be said that a serious attempt is being made to meet this need through what is called "clinical training," when (during the summer or long vacation) theological students go to work in hospitals under expert supervision and learn at least the fundamentals of mental sickness. We learn much about the normal from the abnormal, of course, and all this is of great value. But I do submit that a man will meet a very great many situations in an ordinary ministry to which "clinical training" will offer him very little in the way of an answer. I fear that the present touch of theological students with the "outside world" is much overweighted in the direction of the physically and mentally sick. While I recognize the helpfulness of these studies in dealing with the many who are psychologically or emotionally upset, I wish these same students were in touch with an equal number of healthy pagans! There is no necessity to draw and attract those whose dire need has brought them to a hospital bed, whatever skill it may take to elicit their confidence: but it takes real spiritual and evangelistic power to reach those who do not as yet even recognize that they have any spiritual needs. Too many theological students, and too many clergy, are frankly afraid of people like that, and seldom make any effort to convert them. What clergy need today is more of a good, old-fashioned, God-given passion for souls.

There is no easy solution to the problem of creating spiritual power in our seminaries. The answer will depend partly upon the readiness of the faculty of the seminary to give some time to seeing that, as one graduate put it, the "seminary is a church, as well as a school." This means true pastoral care for the students, on the part of the faculty, of much the same kind as they expect the students later to give to their own people. Example will be worth far more than exhortation here. There are men in seminary classes with all kinds of unresolved problems, the solution to which probably does not lie in anything that can be done in a classroom. There are many problems that will never reach the level of disciplinary matters, but which must be solved if men are not to have a half-hearted, defeated ministry. I believe that, in a day when the mounting paganism of the world about us challenges the Church to be evangelistic in the spirit of everything that it does, the faculty should themselves be evangelists with practical experience, *which continues*, of bringing people to saving faith in Christ. Books can be hide-outs and caves from the reality of life. If we allow professors to become such specialists in their subjects that they feel exempt from direct spiritual impact upon ordinary people, from that very dealing with souls which is to be the main task of their students, then they need not be surprised if later those same students develop specialties of their own, and want to call in psychiatrists or other counselors to do the work which they should have been trained to do. It is not enough, I think, to have one professor of evangelism or pastoral theology who tries to keep in touch with living, breathing, needy souls out in the stream of life—*all* the faculty should have such touch, and if they did it would go far to relieve the academic aloofness which characterizes some seminaries and gets into the blood of their students. In my own seminary days I welcomed the chance to get out on week ends into parishes and schools where I could try out some of the things I was learning: it taught me some things the professors never mentioned, and it added greatly to my ability to sense what was vital to my own ministry in the things they did mention. If I had not had a pretty real spiritual experience before I got there, I never should have guessed that this was a desirable prerequisite to entering the ministry. So far as I remember, nobody said so. And you can't take things like that for granted.

As to the clergy today, when we are, as Thomas Merton says, "living on the doorsill of the apocalypse," what should we be doing? We all know two things: we must keep up the institutional life of our parishes and of the Church; *and* this is by no means sufficient of itself. We know that often we are trying to nurture people in a life they have never decisively begun, which is like trying to train children before they are born; and this means that what is needed is conversion and rebirth for thousands of our ordinary church people, as well as for the thousands on the outside. At the great mission conducted by Bryan Green in New York in the autumn of 1948, when forty-two thousand people filled the Cathedral of St. John the Divine throughout the eight evenings, it was mostly the church people who came and who were converted. *Laus Deo*—it was meant for them first! Unless the Church is converted, the world will never be. We must "begin at Jerusalem." And conversion simply must begin with the clergy. When Bryan Green called for open decisions, there was more than one of our clergy who stood up; and this was no perfunctory thing—there is a vital change amongst our clergy and people which is showing itself in more humility, greater co-operation, and a new spirit of unity throughout the diocese. If this can happen to the Episcopal Church, in the city of New York, through the vast Cathedral of St. John the Divine, there is hope for everybody. And that is the place to begin—with ourselves.

A young man in the ministry writes, "There is only one big problem—myself. All the others stem from this. I was prepared to meet sin in the Church, in every parish; I was not prepared to meet it so persistently in my own life. I was told about the secularism of the modern world; no one told me of the secularism of the clergy who look at their parish problems as though God did not exist, and who try to solve them without Him. Our job is not to be first of all great preachers or pastors or teachers; we are called first of all to be Christians. Prayer is obviously our greatest resource."

In the long, slow sanctification of our souls, I think we need to put more emphasis upon the frankly supernatural aspect of the Christian life and of the Christian ministry. In one way, of course, the Church is harmfully affected by our human frailties. But there are some things in the Church which come to us clear and untarnished from Christ Himself: the Church's own regality as His Bride and Body, the grace that is always there for us in the Sacraments, the "Word" that is within the word of Scripture and feeds the souls of men, the power of God that comes even through the preached word and is more dependent upon the openness of the human channel than upon his cleverness, the whole sheer power of God to "come through" the Church to people in His old, appointed ways. All mere men are partial and fallible; therefore we must not, as someone said, "be disciples of disciples, but be disciples of Christ alone." We must learn all we can from one another, we must be bound to one another in the fellowship of the Body, we must (as S. Peter says) "be subject one to another, and be clothed with humility"—it is only as we are open to the light that is in each other that we learn what humility is. But all of us need to be "subject" to the Church itself much more than we are, then we shall not go astray in putting too much store by human leaders. "One is your Master, even Christ; and all ye are brethren."

It is my belief that we are living in a day when, if we would stir up the fires within us, orthodox Christianity might come into its own. There is a growing reaction, both against watered-down liberalism within the Church, and against the cults and fringe groups that flourish outside the main stream of the Body of Christ. It is astonishing to discover how deep is the search for a real theology on the part of many college students who are concerned with religion at this time; and a man with a shallow sweetness-and-light message simply cannot satisfy them. The Protestant Church will do well to discover and emphasize more and more the Catholic elements of its tradition, without fear or apology; and the Catholic Churches need to discover and emphasize much more their Evangelical elements. The Faith hangs together in one great whole, as you find it in the Creeds. The private interpreters trail off into vagueness, and have their reward. There are tens of thousands of people who are not satisfied with the subjective sentimentalities of the cults, and who cannot swallow the pretensions of Rome, who yet want to domesticate their spirits in a *real Church*, that knows its own mind and offers the whole Catholic faith that has always been the faith of the Church. They are tired of novelty, tired of subjectivism, tired of eclecticism. If we who hold to the faith of the Bible, the Church and the Creeds, only knew what we have, we should sweep the world with it.

Yet the basic answer, for us all, does not lie in emphases and points of view and methods: it lies in a profounder surrender of ourselves to our Lord, in a deeper discovery of His power to guide and use us, in a richer and simpler fellowship amongst ourselves, and in a life and ministry that is converted and converting.

I should like to express my thanks to several of my friends for helpful suggestions concerning this book, without in any way involving them in responsibility for it; the Revs. Dr. John Oliver Nelson, Prof. Wayne K. Clymer, John M. Mulligan, and Sidney W. Goldsmith.

If there is a God-given word or thought in this book that turns a student of theology more deeply to His Lord, or a word of encouragement that helps a man in the ministry of the Church to richer faith and more effective impartation of it to others, it will have served its purpose.

S. M. S.

The Church Alive

CHAPTER ONE

What Is Our Job?

WHAT is the job which we should be doing in the ministry? In a day when specialization has invaded every profession, there is a danger that a man be one-sided in the ministry; but there is also the greater danger that he is cumbered with so many things that he becomes a jack-of-all-trades and does no one thing really well. Unless he finds the one central aim that guides him in all his lesser decisions, he will tend to scatter his shot and fail to do what he was called into the ministry to do.

There are several fields in which he must learn to be reasonably proficient.

He is an *administrator:* he is the executive head of a corporation, and he must know something about the dispatch of business, about the physical fabric of the plant, about construction, maintenance, insurance, investment, etc. Otherwise all this is left in the hands of the governing trustees, and you get the laymen attending to the business, and the clergyman attending to the spiritual part of the parish, which forms a dichotomy that is not intended to exist: there are laymen who think you can run churches like any secular organization, and clergy who know so little about management that they are impractical. Says the rector of a large city parish, "In our administrative structure, the Church is harmed when it becomes clergy-dominated or Vestry-dominated. If it is either of these, there will never be a Vestry meeting which is not bogged down in the treasurer's report or manages to get beyond to the real business of the Vestry which is the spiritual life and health and work of the parish."

He is also a *pastor*. The people are *his* sheep, and he is *their* shepherd. He will not go far wrong if he remembers that at all times. Some sheep are white, some are black, some are a bit soiled—but they are all sheep, and the Great Shepherd loves them and wants them really in His fold. The minister should be concerned in all that concerns them, living his life into them, avoiding the extremes of spoiling them and neglecting them. He should be accessible to them, easy to reach by phone or message, ready to go to them where there is special need, and making his parish rounds regularly and systematically. He ought to have a book with their names and addresses and 'phone numbers in it, and it should be in his pocket most of the time, so that when making a special call in one part of town he may be able to drop in on someone else who lives near by. Let him pray as he goes, and ask God for love in his heart and wisdom in his mind; and he will bring help to them. A healthy concern for not doing all he should will throw him back on God for fresh grace.

He is also a *preacher*. He must take the great truths of the Bible and of the Church, the great central revealed verities, and let them pass through the crucible of his own mind and emotions and experience, gathering those special emphases which come to belong to him as an individual but never letting them predominate over the truth he has received. He must relate this truth to daily life, make it as pithy and close-to-earth as possible, keep it soaked in prayer for days before he gives it and while it is distilling, and then give it with all the force he can muster. Some men preach with about as much enthusiasm as a railroad agent walking through the train and calling, "Checks for baggage": he will help you if you ask him, but it is not a matter of life and death to him. Well, preaching *is* a matter of life and death. You ought to be prepared and know just what you want to say, aim at it, hit it hard, and then stop. Like it or not, more new people, more untouched people, are reached through the preached word than through any liturgical service however beautiful; and the spoken word has always been one of God's means of grace to the souls of men. Do it the very best you can. Put into it every power you have. God will honour and use it, if you offer it to Him from the time the sermon is conceived till you walk down from the pulpit. And, speaking of walking down from the pulpit, don't forget the story of the parson who had a good one that morning, and was going to "lay them in the aisles" with it. He went up to his pulpit with great confidence, and began to preach—but it didn't go well, he couldn't seem to get it out. Afterwards he crawled down sheepishly and sat beside an old deacon on the front bench, who said to him, "Brother, if you had gone up like you came down, you would have come down like you went up!" Let us never feel any confidence beyond the simple confidence that we speak for Christ, are doing the best we can, and are trusting God to use our words.

He is also a *priest*. From the beginning the Church received from Christ certain Sacraments, namely Baptism and Holy Communion, which were the rites by which people were initiated and sustained in their Christian life. This was not then, and is not now, a matter merely of "spirituality"—it was and is a matter of God's mighty act to the world in giving Christ to be born and die and rise again for man's redemption. It was and is a matter of God's gifts of grace given to man, partly in Sacraments. Of these the minister is a custodian, though they are offered by the whole Church together. In administering the Sacraments, the personal side of a man's ministry gives way to its official side: he is acting as an officer, and not in his own name. This is good for him and for his people: it takes off a man the overemphasis of the Protestant churches on human personality. I remember hearing someone say he had gone to Studdert Kennedy's church in London, one morning when "Woodbine Willie" was both preaching and celebrating Holy Communion. My friend said that the sermon was brilliant, personal, he pulled out all his stops (and he had rows of them!), and was his most forceful, witty, eloquent self. Then he turned and went up to the altar, and there the personal Studdert Kennedy disappeared and a priest of God celebrated Holy Communion.

Yet all these things are means which often cross each other as they seek to converge to an end. What is the end? We have not yet really answered our question: What is our job?

Our job in the ministry is to bring persons into relation with our Lord Jesus Christ, and to nourish them in the fellowship of His Church, and to train them in the application of Christian truth to their daily life and work. Our ministry is to people, to *persons.* It is not to congregations or groups, except incidentally and as means: it is to individuals. If a minister takes certain "attitudes" to public affairs (and he must, for the way in which business and politics are run affects people, and whatever affects people is his concern for he is out to establish the Lordship of Christ over every area of life), yet he must never let this be a substitute for work with individual souls. His primary task, the task without which he is in no full sense a minister at all, is the task of winning and nurturing and training souls in the faith of our Lord Jesus Christ, and in the fellowship of His Body, the Church. This is the central work of the ministry; and in some ways it is the hardest work of the ministry, and the one a man is most likely to neglect for other things. For in his work, a minister is also a man. He feels himself part of the compromised and contingent life in which his people share. The amount of power that comes through him to them depends upon his openness to the Holy Spirit. He may be able to pretend elsewhere, but pretense here is easily seen through, and means inevitable failure. Our job in the ministry is with people.

Churches ought to be islands of personalness in the rising sea of mass-humanity. Collectivism and state-ism promise welfare, but they tend to provide impersonalness and growing imposed controls: more security but less liberty. The prospect is fearful if we cannot keep places in society where people are still people, where the true human values are recognized: and we shall find in the end that only the *Christian* thing is the *human* thing. Everything else which appears to be man's benefactor turns out to be his enslaver. Bookish men, institution-men, idea-men, loveless men, in the ministry cannot preserve these sane islands of personalness which are so desperately needed. Every good minister ought to spread round him an aura of personalness. Every Church ought to be a place where people feel that they matter. All this does not mean that we are indifferent to great sweeping social ideas: the Church in Germany learned too late to its sorrow that it had not taken enough responsibility for the way the State was going. The more personal is a man's ministry, the more clear he ought to be about his philosophy of the State. Human lives need the air of freedom to breathe; but freedom, as we know it, came from Christian faith. Except as we keep the root of faith, we shall not keep the fruit of freedom. One has the feeling that one of the reasons why this mass-concept of people has got such a foothold in the State is that it has already had too much of a foothold in the churches; the clergy have been looking for nostrums, legislative, psychological, educational, that would make it less necessary for them to deal constantly with individuals. It is a false search.

Hear this word from a Church Missionary Society News-Letter (London, June 1949), "Bishop Amritanand gave it as the considered judgment of his experience that the great majority of the Christian leaders in the mass movement areas of India whom he knew were men or women to whom some one somewhere had given much time by way of personal attention . . . the key to every situation is the man and woman marked out by the Holy Spirit as the leader. This kind of person commonly emerges only where infinite time and care and trouble can be spent on the individual." Stack that up against the average bustling parish minister—and does it not say something of why he fails and the Church is powerless? Says Dr. Emil Brunner, "The pastor's study, once the room in which a man humbly subjected himself to the Eternal Word, has become transformed into an office for numerous social agencies; and the sermon is a piece of applied popular ethics as the day requires it. The birthright of the gospel of the kingdom of Heaven is sold for the pottage of practical success and immediate influence." One may question whether such work even hits the mark of "practical success" or "immediate influence," at least for very long.

Our first job is the conversion of individual people. Our second job is their nurture in the Christian life through the Church. Our third job is training them to relate faith to daily life. It is my conviction that we are striving to do the last two jobs and not succeeding very well, because we have not done the first one first. You cannot continue what you have not decisively begun; and you cannot nourish a life until it has gotten started. Our weakness lies in the want of conversion in our clergy and in our people. No wonder we do not convert the world outside!

How, then, does conversion take place? Let us take an illustration. Here is a young man with exceptional capacities for getting things done, a very strong ambition to succeed socially and at his work. His family gave him the normal, and average exposure to the church. At school they called him "chief," and everybody went to him that wanted to get something done. Few young men have so much natural capacity for administration, for generalship. Yet there lurked behind this outward success an inward search and longing which his "activism" did not satisfy. Let him take on from here in his own words: "Mine has been a slow conversion, but one that I am happy for. I have always been a hard worker and interested in activity, often too busy to think really about where I was going. I knew I was going to get to the top of whatever I was doing, and began to develop myself in any way that would accomplish this end. I took part in the work of the Christian Association at school, but it never affected me deeply. I entered a large university with the philosophy of activity and 'go-get-'em,' but realizing that this was big game compared with school. Part of my activity was the Christian Association, but principally because I thought this would step me up in the social hierarchy, though I wouldn't have admitted this at the time. I went out for football managership, and lost the competition by a very close decision. My grades had suffered, so I threw myself into study and did not feel the defeat too keenly.

"It so happened that, right after I had lost this managership, I heard about a minister who was visiting our campus. My roommate knew him and told me I ought to go and see him. I only had a few minutes with him that first time, walking down to the train with him. He was the first minister I had ever felt genuinely at home with. Some months after my roommate and I were in the city for a musical comedy, and I made an appointment to see this minister on the Sunday afternoon. I went to his church in the morning and was so impressed with what he said that I took notes on it. That afternoon we had about two hours and a half. I told him I was an ambitious person who wanted to get ahead in the world, and felt no great need for religion in my life. He said he was ambitious, too; and we weren't in such bad company, he thought S. Paul was also, only he was ambitious for the right thing. I asked him how he had gotten started religiously; and he told me he had run into a man who challenged him to face his life in the light of Jesus' absolutes: honesty, purity, unselfishness and love. He said he had been unable to measure up on any of them, and knew he needed to be converted. I told him I couldn't either, but wished I could. He asked if I thought I ever could do this, on my own, and I said, No, I didn't. He said, 'How about letting God take over, where you have failed?' I said I really didn't know who God was, and for me to surrender myself to someone I didn't know would be just words.

"He suggested I surrender what I knew of myself to what I knew of God as portrayed in Jesus. This seemed to me a fair and logical experiment, and we got down on our knees and I surrendered myself.

Though this still seemed only words at the time, I had of my own free will taken a definite step in getting started religiously, one that I was never to forget. Before I left, he gave me a copy of Stanley Jones' *Abundant Living,* and suggested that discipline on my part would be the only thing that would begin to ground my life spiritually. At times my discipline fell off, and my life during the next few months was not much different from what it had been. I was still much concerned with thrusting myself ahead socially. But I stuck spiritually and was beginning to grow. During the summer I went to a Student Christian Movement Conference, and also spent a month at Kirkridge, where the quiet and discipline helped lead me to a more God-centered life. Returning to college, I spent more time thinking about these things. A ferment was going on within me. I could not return to the shallow activism of the past. I helped to get a large number of cell-groups started on the campus. There were times of loneliness and even despair, about which I must be honest. Toward the end of the year came honours for which I worked hard: I got to the top socially, and the managership came my way, after all. I had to have these things before really finding out that there were deeper joys than mere activity and selling oneself in the social market place. Slowly, steadily the Christian life has prevailed over the other. I have made some wonderful friends in this new life, and read some deep and wonderful books, like Trueblood and Buber and Thomas Kelly. What choice have I but to seek in the best way I can to give this same 'good news' of a new life in Christ to other people, and what else can this mean for me but the Christian ministry? 'In His will is our peace.' "

Let me suggest twelve steps that we may well have in mind as we deal with people:

1. *Need.* Everyone has it, and if you think they haven't you don't know them very well. At least there is need in someone near them whom they want to help. There is deep fear, hostility and anxiety in most people.

2. *Rapport.* They will not open up on their need until they feel confidence in us. We must not probe or hurry; just make friends with them, pray and be loving towards them. Personalities that are meant to mesh do so.

3. *Imagination.* Jesus caught the attention of the Woman at the Well when He said, "If thou knewest the gift of God, and who it is that saith unto thee, Give me to drink, thou wouldest have asked of him, and he would have given thee living water." That is all an appeal to imagination. Some story of a con-

verted person, some witness out of our own experience, may stir the imagination of the person we want to reach.

4. *Problem.* Human need usually focuses in some one problem. You may get an indication of it in general conversation if you are on the alert, and it is better to let the person bring it up if possible. It may be obvious to you, but try to evoke it from the other person. Then talk about it. Do most of the listening.

5. *Sin.* There may not be much light while you discuss the problem; but light may come as the person begins to see his or her responsibility for the problem; if not causing it, at least meeting it in a wrong way. Till that happens, discussion of the problem is often trying to fix blame on another. The healthy sense of sin begins where one faces responsibility for one's problem.

6. *Confession.* This may lead to a much fuller discussion of the person's own part in creating the problem. It will lead back into fundamental attitudes and basic sins. Help him to explore the recesses of the inner life, looking for some wrong direction of the fundamental drives of power, sex and security. Let these come out in the open. The fuller the confession the better the chances of true conversion. Counselors and confessors must be good listeners.

7. *Decision.* Christian decision is vague until it includes particulars, like the problems and sins that have come out. We must help people to make an act of self-surrender to Christ, which renounces all known sins, accepts Him as Saviour, and begins the Christian life in earnest.

8. *Restitution.* People cannot always "let bygones be bygones"; they must go back and pick up the stitch where they dropped it, making right whatever can be made right with those whom they have hurt. We must all be square with man if we are to be square with God.

9. *Devotion.* People need elementary help in beginning daily private and perhaps family prayer and Bible Study. We must know some small books that we can recommend to them, such as Stanley Jones' *Abundant Living*, which can be used devotionally. Public worship is an essential in devotional life.

10. *Fellowship.* This means principally church membership; but it should also mean inclusion in small "cells" where Christians meet to talk over and pray about their Christian discipleship. If there isn't one, start one yourself. John Wesley conserved his great evangelistic results in small "class-meetings."

11. *Application.* There ought to be manifested at once a change of spirit, both at home and at work:

more co-operation, humility, readiness to take a heavier share, integrity, cheerfulness. And later the family and the business associates ought to be drawn along into some kind of spiritual fellowship that will transform the home and the business and fill them with Christian spirit.

12. *Witness.* A real change will provoke questions, perhaps chaffing and ridicule. There's our chance! Smilingly yet courageously let us say what has happened, and give our witness to Christ and what He is doing for us. Words must be backed up by life, but life must also be interpreted by words.

Let me plead for deep, adequate dealing with souls on the part of clergy. "They expect us to understand them better than they understand themselves," says Dr. Karl Barth, "and to take them more seriously than they take themselves. We are unfeeling, not when we probe deeply into the wound which they carry when they come to us for healing, but rather when we pass over it as if we did not know why they had come." [1]

I can but indicate briefly some of the qualities in ourselves which we shall need if we are to do such work. We must love people. We must pray for them. We must enjoy them without being sentimental. We

[1] *The Word of God and the Word of Man,* p. 109.

must have a will-to-love, and not a will-to-power, in our dealings with them. We must keep emotionally detached, being both personal and impersonal. We need a knowledge of what life is—it is not, as Dr. Richard Cabot said, for "pleasant fortune" but for "spiritual training." We need cheerfulness, faith, intelligence, flexibility, moral integrity, patience, persistence, humility, a will to understand and not to criticize, the readiness to listen, and above all a great faith that God can come into any situation, into any life, and bring direction and order and joy.

Dealing with individual souls is the base of creating a sound parish life. People who are simply coming and "sitting" create no real parish, though you must love them along till one day conviction deepens and they may want to come to real grips with Christ. People who simply "work," but do not grow and take further spiritual steps, are the bane as well as the backbone of a real parish. There must go on a ceaseless, challenging evangelism, right in the middle of your parish life, a steady evangelization of yourself and of your own people: it is the only safeguard against ruts and routine and heartbreak and spiritual failure. Dr. Donald, who succeeded Phillips Brooks at Trinity Church, Boston, said, "Our sole endeavor should be to labor for the salvation of souls; that is, the upbuilding of individual lives. If the parish, as a parish prospers, so much the better: if it does not, it is not significant. The decay of the parish is nothing: the strengthening of weak wills, the illumination of dim consciences and the inspiration of hopeless people, means everything." [2] The best hours of the best days of the best years of our lives in the ministry should find us in close contact with human souls, talking with them, drawing them by our understanding, challenging them to further and deeper consecration, joining with them in various fellowship gatherings where these great experiences can be shared. It is not to books and ideas and institutions and programs that we are dedicated: but to God and to people. We must keep clear as to this central passion and purpose.

---

[2] In a letter to the Rev. Edward Lincoln Atkinson, in Charles Lewis Slattery's *Life of Edward Lincoln Atkinson*, p. 161.

CHAPTER TWO

Hindrances in Our Work

I SUPPOSE that every man who is ordained goes into the ministry with at least the hope that he will exercise a powerful spiritual influence. And yet, when many men look back across five or ten or twenty years, they are dissatisfied. They know that they have not only not measured up to their early dreams, they have almost forgotten them. This decline from vision to mediocrity occurs because of accepted compromises which grow into accepted defeats, some of which we rationalize away.

What are some of these compromises? All men are swayed by three great instinctive drives—the drive for power, the drive for love, and the drive for security. Ministers are no exception; and the ministry is not only no automatic protection against these urges; it sometimes seems positively to invite the undue exercise of them.

We begin with clerical *ambition.* A man of normal powers feels his powers. He wants to "succeed," and this may be a perfectly legitimate desire—no man ought willingly to fail or to fail uselessly. The ministry is a profession, and a man normally wants to do well in a profession. And so his personal fortunes tend to get bound up with his professional abilities and his parochial success. This sometimes makes men intensely competitive with their neighbours and fellows in the ministry, driving them on to an increasing loneliness and lack of fellowship. They may steal sheep from other folds if it will increase their own numbers and income. They are on the watch for advancement, and will enjoy being the "fair-haired boy" to the ecclesiastical authority. They will use their own personalities to get what they want for themselves. They itch for preferment, and seek to hasten it without waiting for God to give it, if He wills to, in His own time and way. Let it be said plainly, early in his life a man must decide between the exercise of a ministry of spiritual power, and an ecclesiastical career of success. He cannot pursue them both; and in proportion as he pursues one of them, he must forswear the other. The great spiritual forces of the Christian Church have usually had misunderstanding in their own day and only later come to fame. Those who are ecclesiastically successful have glory in their day and often later fall into oblivion. No man should refuse to consider a call to a larger work; but he must ask himself whether this is a call from God, or merely a temptation to his own ego. Till men are broken to Christ, and learn to submerge their own fortunes in the welfare of the Church and Kingdom (which means the prosperity of the rest of the Church, including neighbour clergy), and are healed of the itch to make a name for themselves, we shall have parishes empty of spiritual force, because such men cannot channel the power of God.

Growing out of this are loneliness and hence "lone-wolfing." The parson begins to include fewer and fewer people on "his" work, delegating duties to others, but not sharing with them in common a great enterprise. He tends to give his family little time, because the family becomes a side issue to his own real ambition. He has little that he can say to a dominating vestryman who wants to control all the decisions, because he is like that himself; nor to a female "lay-pope" who expects to be consulted on all parish matters, because he has no answer for this same pride and independence in himself. Standing before the world as an expert in association, he is himself the supreme individualist and becomes the kind of minister who expects to make all the decisions and have everybody acquiesce. You can have a great "conception" of the Church as the Body of Christ, and of all its people as "members one of another," but this will remain sentimental tosh until something breaks this intense individualism and lone-wolfing, and makes a man part of a fellowship which really is a fellowship. I am sorry to say that there are a great many men in the ministry, some of them amongst its ablest representatives, who have never faced, let alone overcome, this brand of immaturity which likes to go it alone. Oh, we want people around us, of course—we want them as the extensions of our own ambitional urge—they are our "field of influence." But in God's sight they are *not*. They are brethren for whom Christ died, and we can do little for them until our will-to-power is changed into a redeeming humility towards them.

Ambition plus lone-wolfing equals *fear*. Off on a spur of pursuing our own career, shutting ourselves off increasingly from our brothers in the ministry, and even from any deep relation to our own people, as the years mount up and run swiftly by, we develop a great fear of what is going to happen to us. Being isolated and isolationist, no one else is in any position to help us forward or give us encouragement or speak about us to a vacant parish; and so we begin frantically writing to people whom we may little know, begging for another opportunity. There is something undignified and inappropriate in all this for a man of God: if it should be done, it should be done by others in his behalf, not by himself. You cannot speak about such things to other men unless you know them pretty well and they know you. We all need to put in place of our fear of what is going to happen to us a concern for what matters to the Kingdom. If truly we "seek first the Kingdom of God and His righteousness," there will ensue a great security in the will of God, which banishes fear.

Bishop Walter Carey once said he thought the hundred hardest-worked men in England were clergy, and the hundred vilest slackers were clergy. It is very easy to grow lazy in the ministry. There is no one to give you strict, or even casual, oversight. It is very simple to get to the place where you do what you like when you like, finding good excuses all the way. Some men in the ministry do not work, they potter. The simple discipline of taking the most difficult task first, of answering the most troublesome letter, would help to undercut this laziness. A man in the ministry who is too good for "dirty work" ought to be somewhere else. The furnace, the hedge, the floors, the desk routine–none of us is above these things if that is where we are needed. An experienced parson, writing about his last three assistants, says, "They are more enamoured of the glamorous parts of the work, like preaching, than of the routine. They don't like to call. I have had to challenge them over and over about this important part of their work. They like to do what they like to do. One of them loathed what he called 'dirty work'—administrative details, responsibility for the bulletin, the fabric. They were late in getting to bed, and late in getting up: they got to the office late, and would have come later if I had not been there to check on them. I think they arrived without any prayers said beforehand." Now that is a pretty picture of three young men, on their way to becoming ministers of parishes with full responsibility! I suggest some of the professors of pastoral theology spend a little time on this kind of thing—not just telling men what they ought to do when they are ordained, but dealing with them spiritually *now* in such a way that they will not behave like this when they are ordained! Among other things, a man is ordained to do a day's work. A lazy parson is a public scandal.

Directly related to this is self-indulgence in many other areas. Some men read, not with a disciplined view of their work, but just to please themselves. Many eat too much, some drink too much, many sleep too much, almost all talk too much. And, I am bound to say, some men work too much, not taking the day-off a week which keeps them fresh and in good trim. A city parson told me once that he loved to curl up on a sofa in the afternoons and read a book—who of us would not like it? But that is not where he ought ordinarily to be. He ought to be out on foot calling on his people, or seeing them by appointment in his study. And a minister not fully grounded in Christ and finding his true satisfaction in winning souls to Him, who is divided in basic loyalty, will almost always be troubled along lines of sex, with everything from flirting to adultery as the result. There will need to be austerities somewhere if we are to have the power we need to convert souls to Christ.

Another of our clerical sins is cowardice. We may be afraid to take a frankly Christian position which contravenes the social *mores* of the group to which we minister. The Church in our southland often reflects nothing better than the prevailing customs about race, and there are state officials who have taken braver stands than some of our clergy. Let us dare to announce the Gospel in both its personal and social aspects, no matter whose toes it treads on, including our own. And how many of us dislike to grasp the nettle in a difficult situation! I knew a clergyman who was a man of great parts, but he was as weak as a puppy when a thorny situation arose, and would always get someone else to deal with it if he could. We tend to keep the peace by letting a situation ride till it explodes, or till it "blows over." A man ought to see and deal with it before this, fearlessly and lovingly handling those persons and situations that are affected, according to moral and spiritual principles that should be ground into his very bones. There is a type of perverse and trouble-making personality that refuses either to be converted or to drop a parish job that has been acquired: try for conversion, try with love and hope and patience and prayer—and if this is refused, then take the situation by the horns and ask for withdrawal from the responsibility. It is wrong for a situation or a parish to suffer for months and years because of a person who will neither change nor withdraw voluntarily. There is a time to exercise with courage your spiritual responsibility as head of the parish.

We suffer also from a low level of faith. We cease to look for miracles, changed lives, healings, answers to prayer, and accommodate, not to people's capacities, as we must, but to their sins, as we must not. You may have to wait for years to see the change you pray for. Perhaps the only thing that will convince some people that they need to be converted is to let them go on in their unconverted ways till they come a cropper, and then they may turn to you for help, provided you never stopped loving them and never stopped letting them know you thought there was more to come! A brother clergyman writes: "Let a man keep up his doctrine and theology, but more important, keep reading his New Testament until he comes to realize that New Testament Christianity is normal Christianity, not abnormal. The doctrine of the Holy Ghost often remains a doctrine rather than becoming a living, present power in people's lives. The things Agnes Sanford talks about in *The Healing Light* are normal, not unusual. That seems to me the great failing of the seminaries. They give the boys the idea that these things are unusual, almost unreal. How can there be power in the Church if we say that the power of the Holy Ghost is unreal?" Clergy need to be searchingly exposed to the climate of miracles, until they are unwilling to breathe the lower air of institutionalism and pseudoreligious materialism.

The ministry suffers greatly from a false humility which talks to itself, and sometimes to others, in this vein: "Of course we cannot expect to see results. We do our duty and look after our people and preach the Word of God and minister of His Sacraments. We keep up bravely and do not let ourselves become discouraged. After all, our Lord did not reach many, and lost even some of them. Rome was not built in a day. We must be content with small things." Now I think that is a warranted recipe for condoned failure. The apostles certainly expected results, and certainly saw them. The word of witness to our Lord Jesus Christ can never "fruitless fall." If some cannot be reached at once, others can and should be. For us to say about ourselves, and for others to say about us in well-meant kindness, that ours is "a faithful, quiet ministry"—(so *very* quiet in some places, says Bryan Green!)—is a blasphemous acceptance of powerlessness, not to be confused with the true humility which knows that all power comes from God, but also knows that God sends power wherever His servants serve Him with all their hearts and give true witness to the truths of the Christian Gospel.

Nothing will more hinder a man in the ministry than lack of integrity. The keeping of appointments on time is a moral matter, not alone one of manners though that is important enough. Carelessness about money, the running up of unpaid bills, and expecting favours and special consideration because he is a clergyman, can bear a negative witness which no amount of sermonizing can ever wipe out. Give no promises unless (1) you remember them, and (2) you expect to fulfill them. Nowhere does life impinge so much upon work, in no profession is it so hard to distinguish between a person as a man and as a professional, as in the ministry. To be what we seem, to take our own medicine, seems an obvious necessity; and yet, how often do we expect to get away with something! I knew a clergyman who was minister of a large, fashionable parish, who had an understanding with the deaconess on his staff, that if anything he did proved to be a mistake, he could tell people that she had made the mistake and it was her fault! Think of the effect on the woman herself—think of the effect on any who learned of this profoundly dishonest and cowardly arrangement! Let us pray and work for a deep moral soundness in ourselves, a steady correspondence between what we profess and how we try to behave. Example alone is never enough to bring people to Christian faith and experience; but we certainly cannot talk one way and live another.

One of the commonest defects of clergy is spiritual immaturity. It would be expected psychologically that most of us who go into the ministry go into it, in part, to deal with some defects in ourselves—we are human beings, subject to the same laws as other men. And it is not surprising if immature personalities seek the role of spiritual leaders, advisors to souls, experts in living, in order to prove to themselves that they are grown up or are growing up. But the plain fact is that, often amongst very prominent clergy, you will find something very reminiscent of a little boy playing church. Their personalities or their intellectual training have got them out beyond their depth, into places they are not really mature enough to fill. Thus, they will storm and bluster if someone contravenes their "authority," and then become pitifully dependent upon someone else to back them up. You get explosions of temper, at home and in the office—touchiness when people make suggestions or criticisms—timidity towards some, intimidation towards others. A bishop writes, "A clergyman must help people to grow, rather than issue orders." But how can he help them to grow if he is in the grip of a subconscious realization that he has not grown up himself, and almost every move has in it some compensation for this felt defect? I think there are two simple remedies for spiritual immaturity: (1) quietly taking responsibility and seeing it through wherever this is indicated, and (2) letting someone else in on one's life in honest fellowship, borrowing strength and maturity from another till it becomes more fully our own.

I have kept till the last the three greatest hindrances in the work of clergy. They are the lack of conversion, the lack of fellowship, and the lack of prayer.

Clergy not converted? Yes. Not a few men go to

seminary to learn what the Christian religion is, intellectually, and to gain knowledge of what the ministry calls for. You can become so engrossed in this study that you by-pass the primary necessity of an experience of Christ; and the faculty may be so busy with research into church history or textual criticism that they forget to do any research into themselves and their own students. What heartaches and tragedies might later be averted if seminaries really saw to the primary need, that ministers be converted to Christ! In one seminary that I know, a good Mohammedan took the three-year course, passed everything, and was ready to graduate in good standing, when—about May of his senior year—the faculty discovered he was still a good Mohammedan and nothing he had heard had had the slightest effect towards making him a Christian! Theoretically there is nothing against a good Mohammedan taking a three-year course in a Christian seminary if he wants to; but practically what does this reveal about the lack of real contact with the students on the part of the faculty? Some of us are so choosy about what *kind* of conversion one ought to have, so critical of kinds we do not understand ourselves, so contemptuous of them sometimes, that we rule out conversion entirely for many of our people. It is never too late to be truly converted in the ministry, as it is never too late to be converted in life. If it has not happened, "now is the time," whether we be in seminary, or near to retirement. The decisive act of self-surrender is and always has been the doorway and turning point of the Christian life.

Fellowship is not just being with people, it is not just back-slapping, it is not just friendship with a few congenial souls in the ministry who "feel as I do" about a lot of things, and have the same "gripes" and prejudices. Fellowship is a continuous realization that we always act *in* and *as of* the Church, the whole enterprise is organically and indivisibly corporate, and therefore each one of us needs a small company with whom we can let out our real needs and aspirations, from whom we can receive help and to whom we can give it. We ought to have this with a few clergy near enough to each other geographically to get together once a week for personal talk and prayer. We ought to have it with our staff, however small or large it may be—a weekly meeting, not only to plan "the work," but also to realign our own spirits, checking ourselves up and making sure we are in fellowship with each other. We ought to have it with the lay-trustees of the church, and that meeting should have resolution in it as well as resolutions, spiritual discussion and policy-making as well as dealing with business matters only, something that pulls these men along spiritually to further levels and does not merely use them as they are. Too many parishes are a one-man show—everyone else is adjunct. There can be no true parish unity, however smooth things may look on the surface, when this is the case.

And our last and greatest hindrance is the want of enough prayer. We drop down into secularity and powerlessness when we do not keep our spirits in touch and in line with the Spirit of God. Our own daily devotion is the thermometer of our spiritual temperature. If there is one *sine qua non* in a minister's life it is an *adequate time for daily devotions.* It must be set before the mail comes and the telephone begins. For men with families, their private devotions ought to precede devotions with the rest of the family. You will have to fight for this, for everything will conspire against it—extra demands, helping with breakfast, getting the kids off to school, besides the natural laziness of the Old Adam who would rather lie in bed. The devil has won his first round in any man's life if he can steal the time he needs for prayer. We ought to *be* praying men, and we ought to *seem* praying men. Is it an effort for you to get on your knees, say in a hospital ward, and pray by a bedside? Is it an effort to suggest prayer to your fellow clergy when you are discussing with them something of importance which needs God's guidance? Is it an effort for you to say your prayers naturally and regularly with your wife and children? If we keep our work bathed in prayer at all times, we shall not go gravely wrong. It needs long periods for prayer sometimes, it needs a solid half hour in the morning at least, and it needs short, ejaculatory prayer as often through the day as you can manage to think of it.

Let us face all these lacks, and others, in ourselves with all the drastic honesty of which we are capable. Let us list our own special sins. And then let us bring them to God through Christ again, asking of Him pardon for them and cleansing from them, and praying Him to give us a new start with Him in that *life* which must ever be the true foundation for the *work* of the ministry.

CHAPTER THREE

What Are Our Sources of Power?

THE Christian minister is called upon to do a very difficult thing: to bring to bear the power of the ideal Gospel upon the unideal world of men and events. His life is a bridge between those two often widely separated continents. He must have a foot in both worlds, and know them as well as he can. But his true anchor must at all times be in the invisible world. His care of those within the household of faith will be effective or ineffective, according as he is pursuing a job and a routine, or is really in touch with the living God. His impact upon those who are without will attract or repel them, according to the potency or impracticality of his own faith.

Where, then, does a man look for the power to do these things?

He looks, rightly, to a knowledge of the Christian faith, and to the constant learning of it in books. He ought to be full of intellectual curiosity, albeit of a disciplined kind lest he know too much of everything and not enough of subjects related to his main task. During his university and seminary days he should have acquired a familiarity with a few great books, curiosity about a great many more, some of which are becoming his own library. A few great books well known are worth dozens of the little obtrusive volumes that will be thrust at him one way or another, and are not worth his time. He ought to have about him more books than he can read; and a train journey or a few days' vacation ought to see two or three of them in his suitcase. And yet we must remember, all this may be a blind alley. It is not ideas alone that move men's minds, least of all borrowed ones: it is true beliefs and convictions, held in faith, expressed with enthusiasm, clad in well-chosen words and springing from real thought. The common lay cliché that clergy are too much occupied with abstract thought has much of truth in it: we often know the theory of the Gospel better than we know the men to whom we must bring it, and this is out of line with a religion which began when "The Word was made flesh and dwelt among us." Ideas are easier to manage than people: they stay fixed and in place, especially as they are arranged and ordered in books; while people never stay the same, sometimes not even as we left them yesterday. Books, other men's ideas about Christianity or the world or life, may often set our minds on fire, starting things in us, giving us something valid to borrow and go on with: but of themselves these are not an adequate source of power. They are seldom the right source for a sermon. Concrete human problems, and the Gospel answer, is the best starting-place for sermons.

Some men seek for power in one theological or ecclesiastical point of view. Perhaps we are so made that all of us must hold to some point of view, some phase of truth or practice that commends itself greatly to us. There is a very wide chasm indeed between the Protestant and Catholic views of religion, so wide that I sometimes think it all but unbridgeable, save in our common love for our Lord and faith in Him. In a Church like my own, unless we are very busy with sheer devotion to Him and constant care for His people and the untouched folk outside, we are perpetually in danger of a kind of schizophrenia because we try to hold them both at the same time. We must allow, I think, that many of our convictions are temperamental and emotional, and we rationalize them because they "say" something to us down deeper than we can quite explain. Our difficulty is to maintain conviction with charity, and to remember that the other fellow must have the right to believe as he does; and that, when it comes to the favour of God's

Holy Spirit, He seems to bless people of whom we often disapprove, and whose Christian life stems from convictions very different from our own. Many in our day have been much affected by "neo-orthodoxy," and the names of Kierkegaard, Barth, and Niebuhr are familiar to us all. As time goes on, we see that this viewpoint has made a great contribution and has profound insights, but its limitations appear in a strange dimming of hope and paralysis of action which seem to make a convenient screen for unbelieving or lazy men to hide behind. As we take a longer look at all our human emphases on one or another phase of the Gospel, on one or another phase of the life of the Church, do we not see them for the "broken lights" which they are, and remember that "Thou, O Lord, art more than they"? In one lifetime we may see some of these things come and go, make their contribution and fade out of the picture. None of us is saved because he is a liberal or a fundamentalist, because he is an Anglo-Catholic or an Evangelical: he is saved by what Jesus Christ did for Him on the Cross, and by faith. If we remember that, we are less likely to make men to stumble over what we think important; what really matters is Christ and His relation to us. A man with a point of view is not so important as one with a Lord and a Church and a Gospel.

Some men depend greatly for power on *action*. They throw themselves into what they are doing—organizing, preaching, even evangelizing—with all the human force that they can command, and the reflex of this upon themselves is very stimulating. I wonder sometimes where the faith of some of us would go if we did not have the constant spur of action. It takes a long sickness sometimes, or some other involuntary interruption of his work, to make a man face himself and his life and his faith, apart from his work. Our work can be so engrossing as to blind us. Perhaps all of us Americans are inherently "activists" and cannot help it in this period of our development: but we need to be reminded that healthy glands can sometimes create a pretty fair counterfeit of grace, and we can sometimes be carried along by the swing of our own successful achievement so that we forget that what we are dealing with is good human steam, and not necessarily divine Power. This is not to say that we are not meant to enjoy our work, and to throw into it all the human powers we have. Phillips Brooks said, "Count it not merely a perfectly legitimate pleasure, count it an essential element of your power, if you can feel a simple delight in what you have to do as a minister, in the fervor of writing, in the glow of speaking, in standing before men and moving them, in contact with the young. The more thoroughly you enjoy it, the better you will do it all."[1] That is all true. But let us keep the distinction between human force and divine grace.

Another source of power on which some men in the ministry depend is personality. We all know what force personality has: how one man can say a sentence and it sounds like a trumpet, while another says the same words and they sound like a cracked phonograph record—the difference lies largely in personality. One man can enthuse you with what enthuses him, and another could not persuade you to eat if you were hungry. The difference lies in what we call "personality." One is always glad to see a young man of gifts and capacities and personal charm go into the ministry, and one always wonders a little what is going to happen to him. One fears lest he become one of the "personality boys." A man with good looks and brains and drive often becomes popular very early in his ministry, and may be carried too quickly into a position which he is not yet ripe enough to handle. There seems to be a fatal weakness in vestries and sessions; they like to find a "comer" and act as if he had already arrived by inviting him to a task that is manifestly too heavy for him. A middle-aged man,

[1] *Lectures on Preaching*, p. 54.

whose timbers are more seasoned, would have done a better job, and the "comer" might have arrived ten years hence. I have seen many a heartbreak and some downright failures where the criterion of a man's being chosen for a big job in the Church was principally personality, with too little thought being given to his real capacities and the stage of his growth. And there is always the danger that we use personality as a substitute for information, application and hard work. A striking personality can be used for God, but it is never to be looked upon as a primary source of power, and may be a definite danger to a Christian minister.

And there are men in the ministry whose conception of power is of about the same level as that of a ward boss. They keep a file of vacancies, they "get around" and hear things, they have a list of men of their own school and viewpoint whom they want to push in the ministry—and the moment there is a vacancy they write a letter with a recommendation. Such a man is either getting even with some kind of defect in himself which causes him to enjoy being a "king-maker," or he is a protagonist for his own viewpoint and is out to fill churches with men who agree with him; in either case he is a menace to the peace of the Church of God. For a bishop to upset the traditions of a parish by recommending men who he knows will try to change them, or to upset the ethos of a whole diocese to conform more closely to his own viewpoint, is the mark of a somewhat tyrannical child. Nothing can be worse manners or morals than for a clergyman to impose his own beliefs upon established institutions, as if they belonged to him. Let me be personal for a moment: when I went to Calvary Church, New York, almost twenty-five years ago, I found a parish with services not so "low" as I was accustomed to; they are today as nearly like those I found in practice as possible. It is not "my" parish: rather I am "their" minister. I wish we might be able to count a little more upon such common good manners between parishes and ministers. You cannot class wire-pulling and ecclesiastical tyranny with *spiritual* power at all—it is just working off some kind of unresolved conflict.

What, then, should be our sources of true power? Where shall we look for the spiritual light and energy to accomplish something of this task which is manifestly too big for us? I think there are four such sources.

The first is Jesus. The most Christian position is the one that lays the greatest emphasis on Him. On Him—not just as an instance of Christian living, even at its supreme and unique highest—but as the Source of the whole stream of Christianity in the world. He is not simply the "best" among many seekers and sages, standing higher than they, but yet of the same basic class: He is the Light in the darkness. Unless He is what we wait for and look for, we are to date without hope. Unless He is the true revelation of God, we have no truth about God and life of which we can really be sure: all other men are wonderers and guessers, as we ourselves are. It is not that mankind, in its tremendous aspiration after God, brought forth Jesus: it is that God, in His tremendous love for man, let Jesus down into the world out of heaven, to be seen and known by us. Until and unless we are clear on this, let us not venture to be Christian ministers at all: for this is the Christian claim and revelation. Our first witness is to Him, as the divine Son of God and Saviour of the world.

Are you clear about His divinity? A while ago, at a conference for theological students, I met a young man who was somewhat perplexed and bewildered. He said his course was meaning little to him, he had no power and did not see much light ahead. Some men's problems are moral: his was a defective and inadequate faith. To him Jesus was just another prophet and religious leader. I said to him what I say to nearly everybody else when we get on the subject of His divinity: "What are you going to do with a

Man Who says of himself, and allows others to say of him, such gigantic and stupendous things—'Come unto me, all ye that labour and are heavy laden, and I will give you rest,' 'All power is given unto me in heaven and on earth,' 'He that hath seen me hath seen the Father,' 'I and my Father are one'? What do you make of it that He commends Peter for his colossal confession, 'Thou art the Christ, the Son of the living God'? If anybody said that about you or me, we should have had the humility and the decency to deny it instantly as blasphemy: but He not only did not deny it, He told Peter that 'flesh and blood hath not revealed it to thee, but my Father which is in heaven.' And He went on to say that He would build His Church on that confession, and He did—and the only churches that are not reproducing themselves and going ahead, according to Dr. K. S. Latourette's great study,[2] are the churches that do not accept this view of Him. It is evident that He believed these things of Himself. How will you interpret this? I think there are three possibilities: He was deceived about Himself, or He was deliberately deceiving others, or else He was what He said He was. He does not behave like a paranoiac to me, nor does He act like a pretender. We are left with the old dilemma on our hands: He was mad, or He was God." This young

[2] *Advance Through Storm*, pp. 481–2.

man listened intently. He had not known Christ after this fashion. He knelt down and made a new commitment of himself to his Saviour and Lord.

Returning home he wrote me, "I sincerely committed my life to the care and direction of Jesus Christ that afternoon. I felt as though I were a doubting Thomas. But His ear was open to my cry. I shared my experience with my good, patient wife who has had to look at me while I tried to live out what seems to me to have been a pseudoChristian life. We have been, up to now, more or less spiritually independent. Never before did I have such grace from God to be so frank about my futile, superficial relation with God. I'm glad I could give away to her what I have found, and we are most happy to share our Christian experience from now on. Preaching the following Sunday, I felt for the first time in my life the power of the Holy Spirit. Then God let me witness last Friday to two philosophy students in the university near by. They were in the library and I checked some books on philosophy for them. I asked if they thought that philosophy was the answer to the world's problems. They said they did: then I told them I believed Christ was the only answer. We talked on in this vein. Some other boys who had been at the retreat with us came in later and chipped in with their contribution. The benefit of the experience was twofold: it gave some of our boys here a chance to see a witnessing situation, and it helped the philosophy students. This experience was one of the most exhilarating I have ever had. We must make sure the values derived from the retreat will not atrophy through disuse. Several of the boys are still steamed up about this new-found discovery of the Holy Spirit. I am concerned that we spread the knowledge of Christ to some of these university students. This ought to be our field while we are here. Pray for us and our development." That, I must add, is the kind of experience which I think would focus a theological student's study in channels of spiritual power, and keep him from deferring his experience of channeling the power of Christ till some later day: would that it might come to thousands of theological students while they are still in seminary!

The second Source of power is the Holy Spirit—as that man found in truly finding Christ. Jesus said, "Ye shall receive power after that the Holy Ghost is come upon you; and ye shall be witnesses unto me both in Jerusalem, and in all Judea, and in Samaria, and unto the uttermost parts of the earth." (Acts 1:8). The revelation was not finished when Jesus came and died and rose and ascended. There was more to come. The Holy Spirit was identical with Him, yet differentiated from Him. Whatever the mysteries of the Trinity, the Holy Spirit represented a new era, a fresh grant of power to the believers of the early Church. How many in the Church today are strangers to that power! They do not even know there is such power, and resemble the Ephesians of old who had "not so much as heard whether there be any Holy Ghost." (Acts 19:2.) It looks as if, before the coming of the Holy Spirit, they had belief and dedication and conviction, but not "power" in this supreme New Testament sense, which is almost always directly associated with Jesus or with the Holy Spirit.

How does one really come in contact with the Holy Spirit? We must first learn about Him, studying what Jesus said and promised concerning Him, and what the New Testament teaches: this will fill our minds with sound and adequate truth about Him, from the revelation in Scripture itself. Then we must begin praying to Him, asking Him to come to us where we are; and that usually means conviction of sin. Jesus said the Spirit would come to "convict the world of sin." We must not think of Him as a celestial policeman, poking out human mischief wherever He can find it: but rather as the Agent of God, trying to help us find out what is the matter with us. Ask Him, therefore, to be definite with you, pointing out the places where you are not pleasing God now. Write them down, and then hand them over to God specifically, one by one. Only He can throw light into the dark corner, and only He, the Comforter (the Strengthener, it means), can give us the capacity to let go of that one great thing, or several things, which stand between us and the power of God.

We find the Holy Spirit, also, in the Christian company. If you go into a Christian gathering critically, saying, "Well, He certainly is not in that parson, or that layman," you will probably not find Him. But if you go in prayer, and immerse yourself in the company, remembering that it is not just this little congregation in the white church on the hill, or the stone edifice on the corner, but the great Holy Catholic Church throughout all the world, to which you belong, and in which you are immersing your little individual life, then you may grow still, and there may come to you a growing sense of His Presence, dealing with you and the rest of the company as effectively as your degree of faith and surrender will permit Him to do. As He comes to you more and more, through the formal services of the Church, and through the informal gatherings of the fellowship, you will begin to inherit some of the "gifts" which He gave to members of the early Church and has given to people in every age since, when they sought Him. Those "gifts" are always manifestations of His power for somebody's help and benefit, through somebody's faith and prayer. We are not yet power-filled Christians till we have moved up through the Crucifixion and the Resurrection and the Ascension, into and beyond Pentecost. The Holy Spirit is the Christian's great present Source of power. He keeps pointing out the thing that needs to be changed, and He keeps pouring out help and strength to change it. He keeps coming through fallible men and women with power that is miraculous.

The third source of power is the Bible. After a man in seminary has learned to dissect the Book into its various parts, and studied the various books critically, he runs the grave risk of going to the Bible with only an historical interest in his mind, or with the pressing homiletical need of a text for next Sunday bearing down upon him. It is not thus that great sermons are made; but this is in any case a wrong attitude towards the Bible. We need steady, daily exposure to the Bible for the growth of our own souls. Let us follow some official lectionary, or lay out for ourselves some orderly method of studying it. Knowledge ought to help devotion, and a good commentary may amplify our private study. But what I am pleading for here is a Bible-reading, Bible-studying, Bible-loving ministry. If out of such study there come thoughts for sermons, they will probably make the best sermons we shall ever preach, for expository preaching still feeds human souls as no other preaching does. There is, however, a vast difference between a fevered fingering over the pages of Holy Scripture seeking a text or sermon for this week, and the deep dwelling within those pages, letting God speak again and again to our souls through them, which should be our constant practice, making the Bible one of our supreme sources of power.

The fourth source of power we have already suggested: the Christian fellowship, the Body of Christ. When Peter stood up to preach at Pentecost, the rest of the apostles stood up with him. We may believe they all would have spoken if they could have done so without confusion: but Peter spoke for them all. They did not say, shyly and irresponsibly, "Oh, leave it to Peter—he'll do it." They did it *with* him, and he did it *as for* them. Ever since those days, no real Christian ever acts purely alone: the company is behind him. He speaks and acts as of the company. When you are "born again" you are born into a family; and that family is the Church. If you take your whole family out for a walk, you will have to go a little more slowly if there are little ones with you who cannot move so fast as you can. In your human family there are adults who must take more responsibility and leadership. These things are true of the Christian family, the Church. People do not belong to it because they are perfect, they belong to it because they want to become more perfect, more like Christ. It is my conviction that some of those who talk loudest about the Church do not always understand it, in the deep, organic sense: it is still too much their "club" or their party's outfit. Others have a mechanical view of it, as if you could latch on to apostolic power by attaching a kind of ecclesiastical pipe-line to the main branch. For yet others the Church is so vague and amorphous an affair that it means little or nothing except a humanly contrived convenience for those who would like to be Christians. But for those who really know and love the Church, not just its outwardnesses, but its holiness because it is the Body and Bride of Christ; and who know one another in Christ through the fellowship of the Body, the Church is one of the indispensable sources of power. None of us is sufficient without God to do the things we are set, as ministers, to do; neither are we sufficient without each other. We must ever be of two minds about the Church. Towards the human and fallible within the Church, we must be critical and seek to convert it, beginning with ourselves. But towards the divine and the God-given in the Church, we must be humble and receptive, seeking to let God's grace find us through this appointed means.

Let any man who knows that he lacks power seek it in these four ways, with diligent prayer; and God will reward his search with His gift of power.

CHAPTER FOUR

Discipline

A CLERGYMAN once said to me, "Whatever I am doing, there is always with me the troubling thought that maybe I ought to be doing something else." Few of us there are who have not been in his situation, and who do not border on it many times in a week of work. Yet this state of mind is a warranted recipe for inattention to what one is doing at a given moment, and could be prelude to a crack-up unless we find an answer for it. That answer lies, I think, in the discovery of *spiritual discipline.*

When the average man goes to his business office, it is likely that his duties get funneled to him in such a way that he has to meet them as they come: it is mostly "laid out" for him by someone over him. In the ministry it is not so. There is no one but ourselves to say at what hour we shall arrive at the office, or to check up whether we get there on time or not. No one will be much the wiser if we duck the difficult problem, or take a couple of hours off to read a novel, or moon about in a haze for half an hour or more, wondering what we should begin with.

Now the thing we should really begin with is a rule of life that includes at least a half hour of personal devotion as the day starts. For me, all discipline starts there, and succeeds or fails there. That gives the "set" to the day. There are usually four elements in an effective early-morning time of devotion: (1) Some plan of worship and prayer, such as you find in Morning Prayer in the Book of Common Prayer, which is regular and repetitious but excellent as steady discipline; (2) Some plan of Bible study, like the lessons of the Prayer Book lectionary, or some other; or a personal plan of studying one book at a time with a good commentary, like Gore's or Dummelow's, if they will help to understand the situations we confront in Scripture; (3) an auxiliary devotional book—a classic like Fenelon or Pascal or Thomas à Kempis—or a contemporary classic like Thomas Kelly's *Testament of Devotion;* and (4) a time of waiting on God in quiet and silence, talking with Him, letting Him talk with us: a spiritual notebook in which to record and so remember what has been "given" to us in this time of silence will be of great assistance. At this moment, as I write, a serious decision has had to be made: it was not clear until a few hours ago, when

I was praying about it, but piece by piece the answer seemed to be given to me in what I believe are God-inspired thoughts. We may need times all through the day when we hark back to one or more of these four means of devotion; and especially in our prayers when the day is done. But much of the effectiveness of "spot" prayer throughout the day is, for me, dependent on what kind of personal devotion has begun the day.

We must seek discipline of *time*. This does not mean that we must be ever in the grip of the next thing, nor that we can always, or even often, order our day ahead of time in such a way that we know at nine in the morning what we shall be doing every hour till ten at night. The ministry is a tension between ordered routine and constant interruption; and the disciplined minister is the one who knows how to meet the one and not miss the other. I know men who set themselves long hours for uninterrupted study and writing of sermons: sometimes there is a deadline and you must cut out interruptions. But such men are in danger of being, not too slack in their schedule, but too rigid, too remote and hard to get at. I think more interruptions allowed might give them better material for their sermons. The late Dr. Henry B. Wright of Yale told me that when he was writing and there came a knock or a call, if he did not meet it, he might sit there wondering afterwards whether it may have been someone thinking of suicide; while if he went and saw the person and found out, it might lead to fifteen or twenty minutes of conversation then, with more later; but it often provided him with just the illustration he needed in his writing! One must exercise judgment here; but I do not find my sermons lose anything by having to take down the telephone now and then when I am writing. We can be selfish about discipline. And sometimes others can be selfish in breaking in upon us needlessly. To plough away at the mail, the administration, the routine that must be done; and yet to be gracious and leisured and open to the person who drops in, thinking no parson has anything to do between Sundays—that is the art we must learn and practice. When he is on duty, I do not see how any parson can consider that he has any time "to himself." He must be busy all the time, yet never be so busy that he seems to his people or his family to be running like a machine. And he must know when to go into a low gear and take plenty of time for some one person or family, building something with them that can never come in a ten-minute call. The discipline of time does not lie in the schedule, it lies in the man.

We must be disciplined about *work*. Why don't colleges and seminaries teach a man how to do a day's work? I think some clergy get away with murder, when it comes to how little they accomplish. One bishop says that he needs, and all clergy need, a job-analysis of what they are supposed to do and how they are measuring up to it. He says, "One reason for the relative innocuousness of the average parson or bishop is his failure to know what he is supposed to do. Not even his people know that, and are all too often satisfied by a man whom they admire for his sincerity and like for his pleasant personality. These would be utterly unsatisfactory criteria for a surgeon to operate on one's child." He must get it clear that his work is to convert people to our Lord, to build them up in Him and in fellowship with each other, and to get them to live out His Spirit and apply His principles in their homes and daily tasks. Everything he does ought to converge towards this supreme end. If it does not, the stream will lose itself in a hundred bogs and marshes of irrelevant side issues. This involves the willingness to spend oneself in detail and hard work. And unless he is himself a worker, not a drone, he will always be finding excuses why he doesn't get things done. One man of considerable ability has been content to stick in a very small parish for many years, because he says frankly he is lazy and enjoys it there. I don't think that's good enough for any Christian minister. The quality of a man's life, and the Christlikeness of his spirit, are more important than the volume of work he turns out; but think back to Jesus, with three years or less in which to get His work rooted and begun in this recalcitrant old world —and consider the astonishing achievement He made in that short time. Let us pray for His quietness and serenity: but let us pray also for His intense concentration, His capacity to move the hearts of men by the life He lived, by the deeds He did, by the work He accomplished.

Then there is a discipline of *tongue* that clergy greatly need. We are men of words, beginning with "the Word." Our worship, our speaking, our contact with people, all depend on words. Words are such sacraments for God to use when they are right, and such pitfalls when they are wrong. We all know we should not gossip and say and pass around unkind things about people; every minister must know how to parry questions born of curiosity concerning his people. Confidences are given him that come to no one else: he will soon forfeit this confidence unless he keeps it inviolate. The problem is to say the given word that God inspires us to say. People need words of comfort and of solace, and will look to us with pathetic eagerness for a word that will help interpret their tragedy and bring them light and more peace. People sometimes need words of challenge and sometimes even of rebuke, words which may put a distance between us and them for a time: such words must be carefully chosen, spoken without anger, yet without fear either. More souls have been damned, I think, by clergy who see people's needs but do not have the courage to go to the mat with them, than by clergy who have been too plain-spoken. We are meant, as someone said, to "comfort the troubled and to trouble the comfortable." Too much talk, loose talk, too many stories, too much chiming in at the common level of conversation and not daring to lift it, too much taking the center of the stage ourselves—we clergy must watch these things as men who must give account of every idle word we speak.

We need to be disciplined about our *money*. Some would say, "My salary sees to that." But it is not so. I have found that people with little money can be both stingy and overlavish. One parson says the bookstore is his saloon! We have our hobbies and our indulgences. Some men let bills pile up at the local stores, till every bit of witnessing they can do for Christ by their words in the pulpit is undercut by what they do to the tradesmen by their deeds in the village. The financial difficulties of the parish, and of the Church at large, would be almost entirely overcome if all Christians gave one-tenth of their income to God's direct work. If we are to expect our people to give in such proportions, then we must give that way ourselves. Do we? If we beg off, they will: if we have faith about it, they will. We have no message for a money-crazy age, or for a nation that cares nothing for balancing its budget, unless we balance our own, and are good Christian stewards in the bargain.

The most important place to be disciplined is *in our own homes*. Discipline about prayer, time, work and tongue—they all come to a focus in how we live at home. If a man is blessed enough, as I am, to have a converted wife who is with him to the hilt in his spiritual work, all this will be much easier; and the climate of the home will depend upon the kind of fellowship the parson and his wife have, and the kind of family devotions they have with the children. This is not easy, either when the children are babies or after they are school age; but with enough purpose, family devotion can be managed. Bible stories told in ways little ones can understand, prayers into which they can enter, a chance to say their own little prayers or verses, enliven family prayers; so does conversation about family problems, followed by prayer concerning them, and waiting upon God for help in solving them. The kind of discipline in families that comes from father or mother "laying down the law" creates rebellion and turns many children later from religion; but the kind of discipline that arises from everybody trying to depend on God, and find His plan for the day, for their lives, for the home, makes of religion a creative and common adventure. Children will go through periods of resistance, and should not be too much forced, but rather lovingly drawn back into the family circle at prayer and devotion.

Perhaps this is the best place to speak about the *clergy and their wives*. Parsons are only human beings, and they like to feel that their marriage is a private thing, which is their business alone and that of the woman they love. They have it neatly arranged: the church is business, the wife and home are personal, private. They will keep the two separate, they say—it is better so. That sounds all right theoretically; the only trouble is, it won't work. In no job in the world is it so impossible to separate life and work as in the ministry. You cannot be a Christian in your ministry and just a "natural man" in your marriage and home. A wife is not a curate, that is true; but you had better have it out with any girl before you marry her, whether she joins you in the Christian quest and discipleship, or whether she is just marrying you because you're you, and not marrying your ministry. That can put a division in your heart that may wreck both your life and your work. Do your best to keep time for her and the children—they deserve some of it, and regularly if you can possibly manage it, and the more relaxed and natural it is the better—but this will sometimes be cut in on by last-minute calls. Unless the whole family is good-naturedly "in" on all this together, there will be frictions and disputes. A man and his wife ought to be growing spiritually, and together, all the time. If they have for any reason begun to grow apart, they will come back to each other as each of them comes more deeply back to God. But if a woman begins her married life to a minister by thinking of God as a kind of rival to her in his life, the augury is not auspicious. A man who truly loves God and loves his wife and lives out his own discipline will draw her and his children along with him, so that there is increasing family unity in Christ. We must not forget: our homes, not less than our lives, are our first witness.

What shall a man do about *intellectual discipline?* Perhaps he can take time in the mornings to get some reading done—frankly, I can't ordinarily; I do most of mine when I get a day off, or during my vacation, or on a railway journey. He ought to take a few good church papers, and keep up with denominational and ecumenical affairs, and some good general periodicals. He ought, as I have said, to have some good big books beside him of secular as well as religious nature, watching all the while for time to look into them. These things should be a kind of background to the use of his personal intellectual faculties. How can he be disciplined about the specific use of his mind for his people and his ministry? Let me make two suggestions: (1) whenever you find a good quotation in a book, which you can use, transpose it to a three-by-five card, and start a filing system for quotations under headings, e.g. Faith, Conversion, Money, Fellowship—a theological library ought to be able to furnish you with headings that would help you do this; and (2) whenever you get a good thought, put it down on a card: it may be a seed-thought for a sermon, it may be a subsidiary thought—but put it down while it is hot, and just as it comes to you—it will perhaps never be as clear or as warm to you again as then, and you can use it later on. Some of the best thoughts come to me as sparks struck off in a personal conversation; sometimes God helps us to say something in a fresh, arresting way to a person right in front of us. If you can remember it, put it down. You will find that doing these simple things leaves you almost never without a dozen or more sermons gestating in the back of your mind, collecting material all the while, and saving infinite time when it comes to writing. I have had dozens of scraps of paper on which were written things that ought to go into this book; then one day they sort themselves into chapters and then paragraphs, and the outline is before you. Don't lose or squander a good idea—most of us don't get enough to waste any of them: put it down and keep it on ice till you need it.

Clergy ought to be disciplined also about *days off*. One of the most hard-working and disciplined parsons I know takes his day off regularly, goes away from his home, walks, reads, rests, goes to a movie if it seems right. Men who go all day seven days a week are often men who are not at their best. I here put in a suggestion that we take Saturday rather than Monday as our day off. Go to bed reasonably early Friday night, and sleep as long as you can Saturday morning—have a good time of devotion, and then get away from the house and the office. Come back in the late afternoon or early evening, look over the mail or whatever has accumulated through the day, go over what you are going to say next morning, and again to bed at a reasonable hour. Then you will be fresh for Sunday, and your people will not be saying, "Are you all right? You look so *tired*." We ought to impart physical as well as spiritual energy to them, and not take it out of them. Taking Saturday off implies that the sermon has been done before, and I think it should have been. Mine are mimeographed, so that the sermon I have just preached is sold in the porch of the church after service; this means a deadline of Thursday noon. You will think of some things on Saturday that you may want to throw in; it is better to have the chance to say them tomorrow, than to wish you had said them yesterday, as you often do when you take Mondays off. Exercise, sleep, food, drink and rest—unless we are disciplined in these elementary things we shall not be disciplined at all. Many a parson wastes time and emotion, staying up all hours, getting up all hours, and always behindhand. Emerson says, "Make the night night, and the day day." A doctor should know us pretty well and keep fairly close tabs on us. The great Dr. Alexander Whyte of Edinburgh said, "Squander your life, but be careful of your health." It is a good rule.

But the hardest of all discipline is the inward discipline that is concerned with *obedience to God.* A young parson writes me, "The life of a minister should really be what it frequently only seems to be: it should be one. Not split up into a theological, and pastoral, and personal part, each of which, depending on the occasion, is nicely put forward to serve as the whole person. He must be one in service, not considering himself dismissed from that service in his personal affairs. I think this becoming one, becoming simplified and simple, can be acquired by more prayer and meditation. This has always been my own personal problem and I haven't found any help in attaining an answer to it, in theological study."

More than any other men, because of our profession, clergy must be utterly honest with themselves. We need again and again—as all Christians do—to face ourselves as we really are. It is easy for us to slip along as if all were well, even when it is far from well. Lewis J. Sherrill, in his book *Guilt and Redemption* (p. 90) says, "The human organism seems capable of enduring anything in the universe except a clear, fully conscious view of one's self as he actually is." Most men have no criterion or method of real self-examination; but we do have, for in the presence of Christ He shows us what we really are, at the same time giving us the grace to face it and the hope and faith to overcome the worst of what we find within us. Our spiritual health lies ever in standing in the white light of the judgment of God. There alone we appear as we are, and there alone find renewal through forgiveness. It is easy enough to face objective truth: the hardest of all truth to face is the truth about ourselves. Let us often get quiet before God, and ask Him to give us conviction about ourselves and our sins. As we kneel before Him, let us say over the old words and let them come presently alive:

> Return, O holy Dove, return,
> Sweet messenger of rest.
> I hate the sins that made thee mourn,
> And drove thee from my breast.

It is all very simple if we will let it be so.

Let the last word in this chapter be spoken to us by that brilliant young Christian, Dietrich Bonhoeffer, who had a shining record as a theological student here as well as in Germany, and was executed at Flossenburg in 1945, just a few days before his camp was liberated by the allied armies. "The command of Jesus," he says, "is hard, unutterably hard, for those who try to resist it. But for those who willingly submit, the yoke is easy, the burden is light. The commandment of Jesus is not a spiritual shock treatment. He asks nothing of us without giving us the strength to perform it."

CHAPTER FIVE

Fellowship

THE Christian religion seems to be of such a nature as to require two things for its continuance and propagation: (1) a formal organization, with fixed beliefs, regulations and methods of worship; and (2) informal gatherings in which people can share their spiritual faith together, wait upon God corporately, and express their faith and fellowship in unpremeditated ways.

It is interesting to know that there were in Judaism small companies of friends who came together for special devotion and charity, within the usual Jewish congregations: they were called *chabûrah*.[1] Jesus and His disciples would in Jewish eyes have formed such a company, and they would have been distinguished from other such companies only by their unusually close bond and the highly independent attitude of their Leader toward accepted religious authority. Such companies often met weekly for supper, perhaps on the eve of the Sabbath or a holy day.

---

[1] See Gregory Dix: *The Shape of the Liturgy*, p. 50.

When it comes to the Christian tradition, it includes both the *ecclesia*, which is the organized Church with its formal worship centering largely in the Holy Communion; and also the *agape*, or informal fellowship of those who love one another in Christ. This is the lineal descendant of the Jewish *chabûrah*. All down through Christian history there have been the ordered gatherings of the *ecclesia*, and also the informal and spontaneous gatherings of the *agape*, or *koinonia*. When I first went to Calvary Church, we began having small, informal meetings; and the then Senior Warden, Mr. George Zabriskie, a man of great learning and an old-fashioned "high churchman," said to me one day, in his precise way, "Mr. Rector, these meetings are not only interesting in themselves, but they are interesting because of their ecclesiastical antecedents."

It would not need much proof if I were to say that the Church as a whole today is overweighted on the formal, liturgical part of its life, and very shy on the informal, spiritually spontaneous part of it. One hears of little even remotely resembling the informal fellowship in the Roman Church, and great numbers of Protestant churches, while carrying many guilds and organizations, do not have anything that corresponds to the early Christian *koinonia*. Let us be clear: the *ecclesia* is *sine qua non*, and no one who truly calls himself a Christian will absent himself from its act of corporate and common worship. The sects which have made so much of the informal fellowship that they have forsaken the formal *ecclesia* have lost something essential. But so, I think, have those churches which have virtually abandoned the *koinonia*, and in which you cannot find a place where you may meet face to face with a few of your fellows, talk informally with them of spiritual matters, pray with them, and find strength in the brotherhood. There just isn't much brotherhood in some churches, and it is one of the lacks which people coming in most feel. My own belief is that the real Christian Church walks on two legs: the formal gathering for ordered worship, and the informal gathering for spiritual fellowship. Other things being equal, it is clearly easier for most men to manage the formal service, and, while they would like to be able to create some small "fellowships" in their parishes, they wonder if these might not "get out of hand," and what would you do if nobody spoke, or if somebody talked too much. And, generally feeling inadequate, they go for more and better organizations, bigger and better congregations and budgets. And the spiritual revival of their parishes waits for them to return to something as old as organized Judaism and

Christianity, and as new as the lift the Holy Spirit gave to a bunch of business men gathered in a hotel whom I met with this morning at 7:30 for a Breakfast Group.

Three groups appear conspicuously in the Gospels: the three (Peter, James and John); the Twelve (all the apostles); and the Seventy (a group chosen for a special evangelistic mission apparently). We do not know why Jesus chose the particular men who made up "the three"—maybe it was because of spiritual gifts and maturity, maybe it was because they were the men of the company whom He could most trust as to judgment and with whom He could most intimately discuss the affairs of His enterprise, maybe it was because He could best impart His most mature and important truth to them. I have the feeling that He both trusted them and needed them. He took them with Him into a high experience at the Transfiguration; and He took them as far as they could go with Him into the depths of Gethsemane. They were evidently His spiritual intimates. Then there were the Twelve, the whole apostolic company, some of them less able to take what He had for them, one of them to turn out very badly indeed. But everyone can see that His early ministry was characterized by crowds up in Galilee, dazzled by His powers and personality and eager to hear His stories and see His miracles, while His later ministry was characterized by more concentrated attention given to these twelve men, eleven of whom at least saw it through with Him to the end, even though his deputy-leader came very near failing altogether. Religion in real power always seems to draw crowds first, and then gets concentrated down on the few who will stay with it and stand by. The Seventy were a third circle, larger, probably less integrated and mature, but in process of being trained by their common spiritual venture.

All of us ought to be part of groups not too unlike these. We need a few people who know us really well, who are all bound together in the bond of some common experience (perhaps a conference or retreat or mission made together), and who will take the time and pay the price of some fairly regular meeting together to exchange experience, discuss new convictions and lay common plans. They become more like brothers and sisters than like colleagues, with deep human as well as spiritual ties, congeniality, enjoyment of one another, resulting. Then we need touch with one or more larger groups, of about a dozen, perhaps consisting of our church staff, perhaps the men of the official board, perhaps other neighboring clergy; in which we both give and receive. This, too, has a kind of long-range quality in it. We take thought for one another, pray for one another, are concerned about one another's concerns. And then there is the special gathering, a week end somewhere for a spiritual conference or retreat, or a mission in which a group of lay-people come along to assist us in the mission by seeing individuals and giving witness themselves. It will not often be possible to keep permanently in touch with all of them, though we ought to be open to a long-range contact with a few of them who are drawn to us and get something from us.

It will generally be found unwise to try to "organize" such groups for informal fellowship. If you announce that you are beginning such a group and ask for attendants, you will get the eccentric and the extreme, as well as a few sound old faithfuls; and the peculiar folk will sometimes give it a stamp that keeps the intelligent people from coming at all. Many of the somewhat odd (whom God loves as much as He loves anybody else) are not best helped by such meetings, but rather by the steady upbuilding that comes through the regular services and work of the Church. The people whom you want most, and who need it most, may be wary and shy of it for a time.

Therefore you need to begin in a lower key, with something that has a generally social flavour and into which spiritual fellowship comes gradually. Church suppers may do it, or these may have taken on such a caste of secularity and triviality that it is hard to get anything across through them. We have found that a coffee hour, directly after morning service, with your faithfuls getting the coffee and serving it to newcomers, and with your best "greeters" getting in touch with them and making friends, is an atmosphere which soon includes the strangers, makes them all feel at home, gives them a half hour of very friendly welcome, and gives us an opportunity to meet and know many newcomers by name. Where possible, without being too intrusive, get their names and addresses on a card; and do not fail to call on them as soon after as possible. It gets them inside the parish-house walls, they enjoy themselves, they meet friendly people who welcome them, and they go away with a pleasant taste in their mouths. This is not quite an *agape*, but if your people and you approach it in the spirit of a spiritual adventure and with a desire to make friends with people whom you may later relate to Christ and His Church, it is a step towards it—a kind of forecast of Christian fellowship amongst some who do not as yet even belong to the Church. In spite of all the "people" we see and are surrounded with, in a great city like New York, there is an unbelievable amount of loneliness in people's hearts. Many of them have never seen, and do not know that there can exist, a

Christian counterpart to the conviviality which most normal people seek, and many try to find in quite other places than churches. Lightness, friendliness, laughter, a pleasant social occasion "break the ice" for many people, and become the most obvious external manifestation of a Church that has a heartbeat in it.

That is what parishes need, and what parishes often lack, a *heartbeat*. Of course, the real heartbeat should be the worshiping congregation, the Presence of God in sacrament and worship. But these belong to the initiated, those on the inside: they mean nothing to the pagan, the untouched, the unconverted. In these days of rampant and widespread paganism, when so many who have been indifferent to the Church are wending their way back to it (sometimes in a rather faltering and zigzag fashion), they will drop in and see what they can find in a Church. If it is all pitched too high for them, it will mystify them—we must not forget there are people all about us today with practically no Christian knowledge, and only the traces of Christian feeling. Everything we do should be tinged and touched with the evangelistic motive, little as we shall use the word directly with those as yet outside. They will look for Christian characters, for friendly people whose lives at least try to match their words: but they will, consciously or unconsciously, look for something else, and that is for people who know something about the right kind of human relations and are themselves in obvious, genuine, loving contact with those about them. The evidential value of functioning small "cells," into which interested people can come, and see God manifestly at work, is incalculable. There is a fine quotation from one of the early Quakers, Robert Barclay, to this effect: "Not by strength of arguments or by a particular disquisition of each doctrine and convincement of my understanding thereby, came I to receive and bear witness of the Truth, but by being secretly reached by this life. For, when I came into the silent assemblies of God's people, I felt a secret power among them, which touched my heart; and as I gave way unto it, I found the evil weakening in me and the good raised up; and so I became thus knit and united unto them, hungering more and more after the increase of this power and life whereby I might feel myself perfectly redeemed. And, indeed, this is the surest way to become a Christian."

What kind of "cells" are there? Let me be concrete: in my parish there are seven at least that function regularly. The largest and earliest is a group of men, mostly business men, who meet on Mondays at 5:30: it began when a clergyman on the staff and the sexton-superintendent met in the boiler room one day eight years ago, were honest with each other about their present spiritual needs, prayed, decided to do it again, and drew others in with them. The women have a group for the wives of men at the men's meeting, and any other interested women, at the same hour. *The Evangel*, our monthly magazine, has a "tea" on Wednesday afternoons, which provides an easy social occasion to draw out some who are there, often with rich results. One of the clergy has a week-night gathering in his apartment, which is largely for training in more advanced steps of leadership and responsibility. There is a group of women who meet on Tuesday evenings specifically for intercessory prayer, preceded by sufficient spiritual preparation and fellowship to get their minds and hearts freshly together before they come to pray. A group of college-age young men and women meet once a week, study, listen to short, relevant talks, share themselves (beginning with their immediate spiritual situation and needs, later telling of ways in which God is at work where they live and work). And there is a group of younger marrieds who meet with one of the clergy, usually on Sunday nights, for study, sharing, fellowship, prayer and planning. I should not advise anyone to decide he needed such and such groups in his parish. All of these have grown up spontaneously, in response to a need, fostered and led by people who have found Christ themselves and had sufficient training to assume some responsibility. We do not exactly want "leaders," in the technical sense: rather conveners, spark plugs, "moderators" (to use the good Presbyterian term for a chairman), who will pray, consult with those responsible for the spiritual life of the parish, do some telephoning, and generally take steady but unobtrusive responsibility for the weekly meeting. Often these meetings are preceded by a gathering of the three or four faithfuls who really care, who come, say an hour earlier, get caught up amongst themselves, wait on God, and seek direction for the day's meeting.

I should say that nearly every gathering in the interest of the Church should have some marks of *koinonia*, or fellowship. It should be natural, at meetings of the trustees or vestry, or committees of them or of the women, to stop and have prayer when a crucial situation arises, or when God's help is particularly needed—and this happens far more often than mere parliamentary procedure will suggest. Business done haphazard is no glory to God; but meetings run as if the Holy Spirit did not exist simply have no place in the Church. It is a pity if some groups in the Church consider themselves "practical" while others consider themselves "spiritual." As body and soul are joined together for this life, so the "practical" and the "spiritual" have need of each other. The extremes of each are the moony mystics who won't turn a practical hand, and the busybodies who are so busy for the Lord they do not have time to pray or keep their own relationships on a Christian level. The thing I am speaking of in this chapter should pervade *all* the work of the Church. The best organization begins organically and remains organic as well as organized.

Whatever other groups or "cells" he may create, the ordinary parson ought to have systematic fellowship with three groups: (1) his own family, in steady daily contact of a spiritual kind; (2) his church staff, however large or small: he should meet them at least once a week, with time for personal sharing as well as despatch of business, and many a difficulty will be avoided if the relations between members of the staff are right; and (3) the local clergy in his town or neighborhood. Let me deal a little more at length with the last two.

First, his staff. It may be only himself, and a few part-time workers—a sexton, a choirmaster, and someone who does religious education. It may be a big city-church staff of twenty to thirty. I have seen staff meetings that were cold routine, colder than some industries, with only business brought up, dominated by the minister, introduced formally by prayer, with not one ounce of spiritual juice in them from beginning to end. That kind produces frustrated staff members, who never get near their own minister in any real way. A tense, hurried executive will scare off his staff and they will never go to him for anything but consultation about their work. I had lunch one day with a prospective assistant minister and a leisurely talk, so that I might know him and he me: he told me afterward it was one more lunch and one more talk than he had ever had with his former rector in two years of working for him. Yes, for him—not with him: there was the miss. Give them something of yourself—your burdens, your needs, your victories, but don't try to keep on top of the heap all the time—let them know that you know your faults (as of course they do). Let your decisions arise out of fellowship and prayer —then you will not only probably make the right ones, but your fellow workers will feel they have had a part in it, and be emotionally geared to getting it done. It is hard not to take a staff for granted. We say to ourselves that they are trained for this: we shall turn them loose and expect them to function. But that means a fission right in the heart of your work. Unless you have a staff that is together, one of them will be undercutting another, instead of everyone feeling real concern for all that the others are doing. And don't let any parson who has read this meet his staff next time and begin by saying, "Of course we have no division here: we trust each other and work in perfect harmony." There may be much more seething discontent under the surface than he recognizes. I suggest he may read the whole last paragraph to them, and then wait to hear the Pollyanna say that all is peace and harmony, and watch the embarrassment of one honest soul that would like to speak up, and say what he or she feels, and would do it if given enough time to do so. Instead of a discussion right here, I suggest some prayer and quiet waiting on God. Then let them say what is on their minds.

Second, the local clergy. It ought to include all non-Roman clergy who will come into it. But it will have to begin organically, if it is not to be another "ministers' meeting," and of some of them many of us are sick to death. You've been to them; there is the lunch, and the resolution to thank the ladies, and the paper, and the desultory discussion, and we go home—starved for the fellowship we did not have. About ten years ago the Greater New York Federation of Churches sought to crack the problem of clerical fellowship in Manhattan Island—almost an insuperable task. They divided the island into "towns." Our "town" was south of Twenty-third Street and east of Broadway to the river. There were some twenty-five non-Roman churches in that area. One of the men invited us to lunch. It was proposed we organize a regular ministers' union. Some of us objected and said what we wanted and needed was a real fellowship, and urged that this must begin by our knowing one another better. That first year we met once a month (as we have done ever since), and asked each man to lead one gathering, telling us of himself, his background, his aspirations and achievements, his difficulties and heartbreaks. Most clergy are afraid to tell one another of spiritual victories (like a conversion, or healing, or other answer to prayer), lest it be considered "crowing" or "talking shop"; and they are afraid to tell each other of problems or failures, lest this set up a trail of gossip and talk: "We hear things aren't going so well over at St. John's," and such-like unbrotherly and unChristian misuse of confidence. We have over the years (for many men happen to have stayed in their cures for quite long periods), developed a real brotherhood amongst us, which issued in a quite remarkable co-operation when it became necessary for us to try to reach out spiritually to the thirty-five thousand new residents in the developments called Peter Cooper Village and Stuyvesant Town, over to the east of us. The fellowship between us has been the gauge of our power to act as a group. It is not enough to try to work out occasional "union services," though these may result, and with us have resulted, from our fellowship together.

I have already referred to the remarkable manifestation of the Holy Spirit through the mission which the Rev. Bryan Green held in the Cathedral of St. John the Divine, in New York, in the autumn of 1948. The real background of that great mission lay primarily in increased fellowship amongst the clergy of the Episcopal Church. We are a very diverse lot, split by differences of "high" and "low," of "big" and "little," and of "colored" and "white." There are a great many of us, and no wholesale method would have worked except superficially. The new unity began when, under the Holy Spirit's impulse, and not quite knowing why we did it, a small group of five clergy began meeting from time to time on a more than usually deep level. Two of them were rectors of large parishes, one white and one colored, one low and one rather high; they were old friends who knew one another well and trusted each other deeply. Another was a recent comer to the city: when we met, we seemed to feel a natural fellowship, and the better we knew each other the more this grew—he is a man with a deep experience of Christ, and a real knowledge of spiritual principle. The fifth was a man I sat next to at a clergy lunch one day; I had known his name, he had just come into the city to do a huge service job which could easily slide down, and at times had slid down, into a pretty secular kind of work. Something said to me, "Get to know him a bit." After lunch we walked uptown, then we walked down again, as far as Calvary Church, and by that time we had grown close enough together to want to go in and kneel down at the altar rail and pray with and for each other. We five became a kind of spearhead, not of official unity, but of actual and organic unity. One Monday morning we met, somewhat impromptu, for two hours of as rich fellowship as you could imagine: I had to remind them—busy men, mind you—that the clock had struck one and some of them might have appointments! Clergy just don't meet that way ordinarily.

Then when there came the Presiding Bishop's call for Evangelism (and it takes a good deal more than a call even from the Presiding Bishop to wake up the Episcopal Church to Evangelism), we had a nucleus that at least knew what he was talking about. And when the Bishop of New York called us all together at the Cathedral one day, and asked me to take on the clergy of Manhattan in the evangelistic program, we had our "team" already functioning. We invited other clergy to come for meetings about once in two weeks. We did not meet only as clergy, but as fellow sinners and as those needing God and each other. A man in whose life something had happened would speak of it simply to us. Another would express a difficulty. We shook off the self-consciousness which so often divides us from each other, and the leaven of the small group began permeating the larger one. We found Evangelism a good common ground for those of different viewpoints to meet on. Gradually the spirit of teamwork and fellowship built up till it pervaded our clergy in the whole city. So that by the time Bryan Green arrived, we had an undivided group of clergy, ready to give it everything they had. It was, I am sure, the kind of unity created by the Holy Spirit in a fellowship of men who before had known no such unity, that was the real background and foundation of the unprecedented diocesan mission and its successful outcome.

How important it is that theological students learn how to create such groups! About a year and a half ago I was speaking at a men's club in one of the suburbs, and there in that meeting God called a young man to go into the ministry. He was in business, it meant going back to college for over a year, but he did it. I talked with him a few times—a quiet fellow, serious of purpose, cautious of temperament. What was my surprise to hear from him, after some weeks at college, that he had got a "cell" started and it was going strong! I asked him not long ago to put down for me what he had learned, as a layman and prospective theologue, in leading that group, and this is what he writes: "Bishop Emrich says, 'Without Christ we live *surface* lives,' which should challenge us to build more effective cells, so that we may not be accused of living 'surface lives.' As to what I have learned: first of all the leader must learn that he must not 'lead.' The only effective cell is that in which all those concerned have learned to rely on the leadership of the Holy Spirit. This is a very difficult concept to put across and one which we can only believe when we have actually taken time out to be quiet and to let Him guide us. Second, we must not excuse ourselves and say that we are not ready, rather we must start where we are. I am sure that God will use those who only stop to ask. We must also remember that the time is now, and that the people around us are as tired as we are of living 'surface lives.' We Episcopalians are not very good at praying, so when I started the cell last fall I read a few pages from *A Guide to True Peace* the first few times that we got together. I think it helped us all to think about the meaning of silence, of prayer, and of the power of the Holy Spirit. Later, we usually read a chapter out of the Bible each day in the week before we came together, as I found it helped the boys to talk more freely. In short order some of them began to make it a daily habit. We prayed for specific things, like the program of our Canterbury Club. One of the boys said he thought too much emphasis was laid on the emotional adjustments in marriage, and not enough on the spiritual. By praying about this with us, he was able to go back and talk with his wife for the first time about his spiritual convictions. . . . Frankly the best advice I know about 'cells' is to be humble, to get started, and to let the Lord take over."

And how important it is, also, that fellowship be not merely a series of gatherings together of congenial minds, but something which pervades and transforms all the work that the Church has to do! I had a letter recently from a friend of mine who is Moderator of his Presbytery, and who describes a meeting of a Committee on Church Vocations. He says, "It lasted all day till 7 P. M. with about 20 candidates present for the day. Morning schedule included personality and psychology tests by our Board of Christian education psychologist, and also personal interviews of each candidate by a member of the committee. Then lunch together at the church, and the afternoon spent with each candidate appearing separately before the committee. They ranged all the way from high school to graduate school. The case of one fellow was interesting. I have never seen a church committee give so much in real counsel, corrective and fellowship. It put meat into the word 'fellowship' within the given framework of the Church. This fellow had finished two years at seminary, had a call coming up in a resort section, and planned to be married in July; the manse was waiting and a summer season in which he pictured the girl helping him in the church. Because of some evidences of irresponsibility, too many girls in succession, and seeming to rush the committee and to be superficial about it, he was asked firmly to put off marriage till later and really get to work in the church, and make this his own conviction in talking with his girl about the postponement. It was most refreshing to see a committee doing it and in such a redemptive spirit." "Fellowship" is not, you see, just a series of meetings, but a state of living out one's Christian love in all one's relationships and letting God work in them.

One last word about the value of week-end or ten-day conferences or retreats. One minister I know, who has a large but by no means wealthy congregation, takes different groups of them away about once a month, to be together for prayer, fellowship and mutual exchange—he says it has proven invaluable. He leads the conference himself: but he is a deeply converted, Spirit-guided man, who knows how to lead without dominating and how to draw the people out in expression of their views and experiences. One may invite in a special leader for such times. The danger is that the leader may talk too much, and not allow enough time, either for silent prayer or spoken prayer which give the Holy Spirit fresh access to the company, or for expression from the people at the conference. A vital gathering is three-cornered: the leader (or leaders, for there should be a small fellowship behind it all), the attendants at the conference, and the Holy Spirit. One young man writes, "Our clergy conferences have so far been concerned with shoptalk of little consequence—more wind than Spirit. If I were a bishop, I should try to nourish my clergy periodically." Now many bishops and other ecclesiastical leaders have such gatherings for their clergy. But too often they are overloaded with subjects and speakers, and turn into a series of lectures with a few questions and answers: they are too highly organized, and not organic enough. What men really want and need from such gatherings is an experience of Pentecost, when a few gather "with one accord in one place," where there is much prayer before and during the conference, where time is given for *something to happen* to the men personally and corporately, where they are released and empowered again by being given the chance to be honest about failures and needs, as well as humbly grateful for ways in which God has used them and to which they give utterance in the fellowship. The bishops and other leaders need themselves a course in how to conduct a fellowship meeting, for most of them dominate it too much, or run it through too much like a business meeting. In fact, there is nothing more needed in all churches today than men skilled in the art of creating fellowship. We know how to conduct a formal church service, we know how to run a meeting of the vestry or session, or to preside at a business meeting, we know how to get up and make an inspirational address on a semi-informal occasion; but we must learn how to conduct meetings of the fellowship, how to throw in enough leaven to set something to work, how to get the small nucleus behind it, praying all the while, how to coax out the shy ones and draw out those with something vital to contribute, how to remind the fellow who is talking too long that we want to hear from others, too, or the fellow who is grinding some personal ax that this is not a forum, and what we want is not so much his opinions as his heart and his experience. Prayer, our own release, humor, tact (which means "touch," and not caution), a fund of human spiritual experiences to which we can refer for evidence and illustration, a genuine love for people, and above all a steady reliance on God's Spirit throughout—these things will help us as we seek to learn how the Holy Spirit still makes Himself known in the gathered companies of Christ's people.

CHAPTER SIX

Some Problems Considered

In this chapter let us take a brief look at some of the questions and problems that confront every minister, and try to suggest lines along which answers may lie. This is an extremely difficult and dangerous thing to do: it would obviously take some courses in moral and pastoral theology plus a great deal of experience to suggest even reasonably adequate answers to many problems. One young minister who knew I was writing this book says, "Don't give us any pat answers—I don't believe there are any." He is right—there aren't any. But there are answers, and we must try to discover them if we are to live out an effective ministry.

What shall we do with people who ask for money? If we know them, or they can establish contact with someone who will vouch for them, or they are stable people in temporary trouble, Christian charity will cause us to make a loan or a gift to them. If we do not know them, and they cannot establish any position of confidence, if they are of the "panhandler" type, there is not money enough in your parish to satisfy them, and giving to them will be pouring money down a rat-hole. The amount of irresponsible money that Christians, including Christian ministers, squander on pathetic-looking ne'er-do-wells, while they fail to support our own missionaries who are often in great need, is scandalous. We all take some chances, sometimes they prove to be right; and we had better be stuck sometimes than be cynical. I try to hold to the principle that, if I cannot take the time to try to make some spiritual and fundamental contribution to the person, I will not put him off with money alone. Few casuals who ask for money ever pay it back, in my experience. If we are really going to help people, it must go beyond the quarter on the street, or the loan or gift made in the office. Sentimentality is no answer. Neither is hardheartedness. Only a real change of heart as prelude to a change of circumstance. We must deal with the person as a whole, not just his immediate circumstance and *his own idea* of how he needs to be helped.

What do we do about a new "call"? Our first reaction should be, "Lord, what wilt thou have me to do?" Then an impartial consideration of the relative spiritual opportunities of where we are and the possible new field. Get all the facts, without tipping your hand, or letting your emotions become involved too much. If you want to go, ask yourself why: "Do I feel unappreciated where I am? Is my pride hurt? Is it the larger salary alone? Does it feed my ego, or contribute to the good of Christ's Kingdom? If I want to stay, is it fear of adventure and larger responsibility, the comfort of less work, the possibly false humility of staying in a smaller place?" We should talk with people of Christian conviction, especially those who know us well, and ask their prayerful advice. I am convinced many clergy wish to advise other clergy *without prayer* in these matters; it ministers to their own self-importance: a few minutes together on their knees would be worth far more than all the noisy talk and advice. God has a will, and He reveals it to those who honestly seek it: "He that willeth to do his will shall know . . ." (S. John 7:17). After all other considerations have been weighed, get quiet before God, perhaps with those whom you spiritually trust most, and in His own time and way He will cause you to "know." Abraham Lincoln said that he found that, when the Almighty wanted him to do or not to do a particular thing, He had a way of letting him know it. Stew and confusion, ambition and advice, may give the wrong steer: but real prayer will show us what to do.

How can we get our people to take leadership and responsibility? One man says the rest let the old "work horses" do it all, and his predecessor spoiled the people by doing too much himself. This is not primarily an administrative, but an emotional, problem: it arises out of the lack of release in the people's hearts. Religion is for them, as William James said, "a dull habit" rather than "an acute fever." You must have the fever yourself if you are to be contagious. Draw people into your counsels about community or parish problems, asking their advice: the person who "warms" to the problem may be the person who will most help you actively to solve it. "Church work" sounds dull and often is. But a problem to be solved or an opportunity to be met, when pared down to concrete form, is almost always interesting. We must know how to relate the local problem to the world situation, so that people feel they are doing something that gears in with a larger program. You need your old faithfuls; but there will be some older people in every parish who simply will not learn the new ways that are necessary in new days. Turn elsewhere: look for the capable younger person who may not know as much about the Church, get him interested through participation in a job that appeals to his imagination. That touches his emotions, and only this will get him "moving." If you are kindled yourself, you can kindle others.

How much time should I take for sermons? It depends somewhat on how easily you think and write.

In a sense you are always thinking about sermons, about subjects and about material. Get your backbone theme, then begin attaching ribs to it as they occur to you. Put down your central theme while it is hot in your mind, with as many subsidiary ideas as "come" to you then. Then get down to hard work. Set aside enough time in the week to write out carefully what you are going to say. You may need to rewrite it several times. Do not trust to a few rough notes, except where you are speaking once in some place: your own people week after week deserve the care of well-prepared sermons, with no unintentional repetitions, and you must know exactly what you are going to say. You may prepare so fully that you can deliver it ex tempore; or you may learn your MS by heart and give it so that it sounds extempore; or you may take it with you into the pulpit having mastered it quite fully, and occasionally looking down at your MS. I find that a typewriter helps me in two ways, as I write sermons: (1) it saves me the distraction of my own handwriting and is much more legible; and (2) it is much easier to gauge length and the relative proportions of different sections when they are written on a typed page. I do not see how men can expect to preach well who leave their preparation till Saturday. I think a few men take too much time over sermons, overdressing them and "prettifying" them and so taking some of the virility out of them. See it clearly—feel it deeply—say it directly—are fairly good rules for preaching.

How shall we deal with the old-minded, ultra-conservative people? The problem is not one of age, but of outlook: some of the old are young-minded and know things must change, some of the young are old-minded and want to take as their motto "as it was in the beginning, is now and ever shall be, world without end." They resent change, and will resist any suggestion that they or the Church need to change. While loving these people and serving them in every way we can, we must not set our practice by their views. While keeping personal and pastoral contact with them, let us go for the younger-minded folk more characteristic of this age and time. We must live the Gospel and preach it. If you say what you ought to say about racial problems, if you say what you ought to say about industrial problems, if you challenge complacent church folk with the sins they have along with all the rest of us, you are going to get opposition. Be sure of your facts, don't be wild in your statements, keep sweet in all your human relations, take the underdog to task as well as the privileged for he has his own kind of sins, don't "take them to a fire" every Sunday morning, but do not fear the face of man. Some men in the ministry become unpopular because they are constitutional jackasses and do and say the thing in stupid, needlessly tactless ways. But some men become unpopular because they really stand for Christian principles. Let us trust God to look after us if our way leads to a cross. I wish all conservative church people could hear what Chaplain George B. Wood, of the 82nd Airborne Division, says of them: "But you can't really blame them. Most of them have nice, easy lives. They've never seen a baby with its arms blown off, or a man in six pieces gathered together for burial. So they just feel that religion is nothing to get steamed up about." Don't—in the Name of Christ I say it—don't be so tactful with such people that you send them to hell in their sins because you did not dare to speak up. Plenty of personal love and pastoral care; and then plenty of salt and fire and plain-spoken truth.

What shall we do with "cranks"? Every so often I have an urgent call from somebody who has a recipe for Utopia and wants the Church to get behind it. Remember that you will find one or two good ones amongst these folk in the course of a few years, somebody with a real idea about something: I picked up an old and poor Quaker saint a while ago and would not take anything for my hour with her. But you must discern whether this person has the germ of a real idea, or is an egoistic neurotic who likes to talk and build castles in the air. If it is the first, some effort to refer them to an agency or cause that is working along a similar line may be wise; if the second, you may want to offer spiritual, and secure psychiatric, help—but you may be embarking on a very long course. You ought to know in ten or fifteen minutes whether to keep on, or whether to stand up politely and edge over towards the door. Such people can take an enormous amount of time which should be going into constructive channels.

Suppose I have failed? I came with high hopes, I honestly did my best, but things have not worked out as I had hoped. Nobody who works with God succeeds in quite the way he foresaw for himself, I think. Some measure of failure is in the cards for us all, for we follow a Man Who failed—failed so gloriously that I think we can say He failed successfully—and that is what we must do. The indication may be a full admission of the situation to our trustees, some prayer with them and honest consultation as to whether we try another tack, or whether we had better go elsewhere. Just staying on is no solution—and God will not let an honest man down; there will be work and a living somewhere if he lives on principle and not compromise. The failure may lie in a defect that we can and must correct: let us go to the best spiritual adviser we can find, and ask him to dig deep and help us to change. It may lie in too shallow a spiritual message, so that people are not being converted. It may lie in the fact that we ought to be somewhere else, or doing another kind of work. In any case, let us call it what it is—failure—and not fool ourselves about it. But Jesus took the greatest Failure in the world and said that through it He would "draw all men unto Him." I know a man in the ministry who failed in his parish: it hit him awfully hard, and he took a while to recover from the blow of it; but he is ten times the man he was when he was successful, and exercising a far deeper influence in a slightly different field. Only Christ can help people to fail successfully.

What should be our own financial giving to the Church? This is a real problem for many men on small salaries. One cannot be dogmatic. Yet I am convinced the only solution for the Church's financial problem is *tithing*, and I do not see how we can ask our people to tithe unless we do it ourselves. The people I know who do it, clergy and lay-people, always say it is a blessing to them, not a hardship. We may feel led to give some of the tenth to other Christian enterprises than our own local church or missionary quota; but we must watch this or we shall penalize the Church. When I see what some clergy spend on tobacco or the theater in a year, I wonder where their sense of stewardship has gone and their sense of relative values. Unless we are sometimes called to "go out on a limb" of faith, personally and as to our parish, I do not see where faith comes in: it becomes just the running of a business with a budget. And I think the first place to begin is with our own tithing.

This raises the whole question of money in connection with the Church. Finances are not one thing, and faith another: money is work, life and caring. Raising it is not "dirty work," but training people in Christian stewardship. We ought not to be thinking nor talking about it all the time, but a man who feels uncomfortable about mentioning it to people, privately as well as publicly, is flinching from part of his duty. You will be shocked and surprised by the generosity of those you know "cannot afford it," and the niggardly indifference of many who can. As I am writing this, two old women, with nothing in the world, have come each with a check for $50: one took it from her burial money, the other from God knows where; and I have recently almost been on my knees to two families that live in great comfort but drop in their small silver when they are in church. Be prepared for this: I am bound to say that after twenty-nine years in the ministry, it still stuns me a bit. The parasites who let others carry them are too numerous. But looked at in the large, let us hold to the principle that "Where God guides He provides." If what we are doing is His work, He will not let us down. He may let us sail close to the wind, take some chances, act on faith; but He will come through in His own time and way. Our own faith about money may say more to people in these uncertain days than any number of sermons on faith or stewardship.

How much time should a man spend in activities outside his own parish? The longer you live in a community the more do you seem to "collect" people and causes that seem to have a claim upon you. If your people are told to get out "into the world" with their Christianity, you must go with them and give them a lead. It becomes a matter of values and of divine guidance. The parish comes first in our concern; the general missionary work of our communion ought to come next, I think; then the work of larger units of the Church—Diocese or Presbytery or Conference—and then other concerns of our communities. Most men in the ministry have a specialty to which they feel called to devote time—religious education, evangelism, psychiatry, writing, etc. When one's outreach grows larger, one must choose a field, or several fields, to which he feels committed, and almost ruthlessly shut out the claims of other things. Merely running about preaching hit-and-run sermons does little good. I sometimes wonder how much good is done by the enormous amount of Lenten preaching that we do. A week or ten days of a real parish mission, under a man who knows how to conduct one, with everybody working and praying in preparation and in follow-up, would do a great deal more than several weeks of noonday services. Your parish is not only your first responsibility: it is also your laboratory of validation—your proving ground for what you say elsewhere. If you feel called to a certain amount of extraparochial activity, draw your people along with you into the enterprise, get them thinking and praying about it. The actual decision whether you take on this or that responsibility, accept this or that invitation, say "yes" or "no" to someone's request, should depend on (1) your long-range commitments, the fields to which you have felt led to devote extra time, and (2) to the Spirit's guidance as you ask what to do in this case, whether it constitutes an exception or not.

What shall we do about the parish organizations we find as we enter a new field? Don't do anything too hurriedly. Take their measure. Some of them are essential, and, even if they are weak, or in wrong hands, must be strengthened and gradually got into better hands. This means for you, and for your more progressive people, a policy of patience and full identification with what the organization is trying to do. It does not mean a sentimental willingness to continue indefinitely something that has outgrown its usefulness. Some organizations are best left to die of inanition, they will take care of themselves in time. Others had better be knocked in the head before they die naturally. Many a parish organization which began with usefulness becomes decrepit in time, and then it is the refuge of a few sentimental and backward-looking people who live in the past and for whom the "dear old guild" is not much more than a club—a club sometimes in two senses, a little society for their own satisfaction, and a stick to brandish over your head if you try to bring in too many new ideas. Organizations ought all to be work groups and also spiritual fellowships. They ought to be places where convinced Christians find an outlet for their desire to work in some direction, and where newcomers, especially those with little church background, find something besides manual activity, where they find people that love Christ and know Him and know how to make Him known to others.

What shall we do if a determined opposition forms? If it concerns some people's dislike of a minor change, something unessential, we can afford to give way on it. If it becomes clear to us that the people were better informed, and made a better judgment than we, we must give way, and do it graciously and good-naturedly. Men who make mountainous ecclesiastical issues out of their own personal preferences, and assert their ministerial prerogative about trivialities, will find they have no authority left when they need it in a big issue. When it comes to a real and important issue, where spiritual principle is at stake, where the opposition is uninformed or obstructionist, it is time to put down your foot. Some of my vestry once wanted to elect a man whom I knew to be spiritually opposed to everything we were trying to do in the parish: I let them talk for a while, and then I said quietly that there was not room for that man and myself on the same vestry, and heard no more of it. Do not forget: conviction of sin can develop in the hearts of some of your best "old faithfuls." Because "the good is the enemy of the best," they will make their "good" the enemy of the "best" that you want for them, and say, like the man in Jesus' parable, "The old is better." If you are preaching and living a real Gospel, there will be people right in your congregation who will not like it and will undercut you openly or secretly. Do not let such people get into the real counsels of the parish if you can help it. Work with them wherever you can, but make plain to them where you stand. And, when it comes to a showdown, stand your ground and assert your spiritual authority. But do not, I say it again, waste an atom bomb on a rabbit:

keep your assertion of authority for the big issues, and do not manifest your own immaturity by displaying it all over the place in relation to small issues. When the issue is between one group and another of your people, the tactful parson thinks, "I will not take sides." Unfortunately life is not so simple as that: he may find that at least more right is on one side than on the other. He must deal also with the wrong on both sides, which may lie in the spirit of one group towards the other. After a while the points really at issue are lost in personal or group feuds—then he must deal with the persons, and with their reconciliation, before he can help settle the point at issue. He had better be mindful of *what* is right, rather than *who* is right. Again, love, firmness, calmness of spirit, and courage, will be needed.

What should be a man's relation to his chief, when he comes to work as assistant? And how should the senior minister treat a junior? Most effective clergy are busy men, and it is very easy for them to take their assistants for granted. I spent a most fruitful year as assistant to one of the greatest pastors in the Episcopal Church, and learned a great deal from him: but I am bound to say, I only saw him when it was on a business matter and when, occasionally after evening service, I would have a half hour with him in his study. I had to pick up most of what I learned by observation. It would have been better if we had had a deeper fellowship. Some assistants are jealous, and become subtly and even openly divisive and disloyal: it will return to plague them if ever they have an assistant and have no message for him when he does what they were never cured of doing, i.e. nursing plain ambition. Some assistants think their chief very unfair when he expects a full day's work from them, or when he does not let them preach in his place (which is seldom possible). An organization must have a head. On the other hand, authority alone can produce frustration and rebellion in assistants: there is needed a relationship in which assistants can speak their minds fully without being slapped down by a chief whose egotism has been offended. The truth spoken in love seems to be the answer here, as in so many other places.

What should be our relation to psychiatry? It is my opinion that ministers benefit from a general knowledge of psychiatry, if they do not seek themselves to become psychiatrists. Ours is a different field. It seems to me we should avoid two extremes: one, of ignoring the gains and insights which the whole modern field of psychotherapy has opened up to us, with the specific help which sane psychiatrists can give to mentally disturbed persons, some of whom may be our own church people—mental sickness, like physical sickness, needs expert medical care; and the other, of going overboard in believing that psychiatry has all the answers, and throwing up our hands whenever we meet something bordering on nervous or mental instability. When you feel you are getting into something that is pathological, that is deeper than your experience can go, talk with a good psychiatrist and if need be send the person concerned to see him. There are psychiatrists who seem to be materialists through and through, and to whom I would not expose anyone. But there are many more who are well-trained, eager to help actual human beings, and fully aware that, when it comes to the integration of personality, and to applying on a permanent basis even the insights they themselves have revealed, the ministration of the Church is almost always helpful, and sometimes determinative. I say "almost always," because there are clergy who are criminally ignorant of the elementary problems of mental health, and these can do considerable harm. If we understand people and are in touch with God, we are doing a pretty steady job of helping to keep people mentally well. Many an emotional and mental sickness begins in our people which is slowly but steadily resolved in the worship and fellowship of the Church. But sometimes the technical psychiatrist is needed.

What about co-operation with other churches? The

first need is for an ecumenical heart and mind, a will to see the good in others, a will to work together so far as possible. The emotional "sectarian" is found in every group, Conservative and Liberal, Anglo-Catholic and Protestant. There are interpretations and convictions, held by individuals and by some churches, which make co-operation at the highest point, i.e. in the celebration of the Holy Communion, impossible. We may or may not share in these beliefs: but we must not pour scorn on them if we do not, nor force them on others if we do. Everyone knows we can co-operate on the periphery, say, of social service; and we ought to do it. But we must bring the area of co-operation nearer to the Center. Evangelism is a most potent field of united attack. There is a trunk of accepted Christian truth and revelation where we can all agree, before we begin going out on our various branches of denominational differences. If you can get a man who will not inject his personal viewpoint, but will stick to the Gospel, bringing to bear upon it reasonable intelligence, he can speak for all groups. After Bryan Green spoke at the great diocesan mission in New York, a very high-church parson friend of mine said to me, "He did not say a thing in that mission with which I disagreed." And I said, "He did not say a thing with which I disagreed. He must have been hitting at central truth all the time." Our own brotherliness and good manners towards men of other beliefs will go far to mitigate our inability to go as far with co-operation as some of them desire. There are, let me be frank, Episcopalians who treat all other Christians as if they were not only ecclesiastically irregular, but socially inferior: and this is an offense to the Master which I think He finds it hard to forgive. Fellowship, open talk where increasing frankness is possible, prayer, working for the evangelization of our communities—surely these things are open to us if we are open to them. Are we?

How intimate should be our relation with our people? The Romans cut that knot and keep the relation official: it is not Fr. Kelley they want, but just a priest. They may love their pastors and their pastors may love them; but the relation is basically official. With us it is not so. We do well to build up some objective view of our office, and to maintain a kind of unpretentious dignity. But we believe in a more intimate pastoral relation. The evangelical churches really ought to *be* more evangelical than the Roman, for we put a greater emphasis on preaching and have a better opportunity of reaching the untouched through it. Preaching, as Phillips Brooks said, is "truth through personality." Both are important—the truth more important, but the truth-bearer important, also. We cannot help drawing people to ourselves, as well as to Christ; perhaps to Christ *through* ourselves. Let us not fear this. We must keep from sentimental relationships, from playing favorites, from using our people; but we are meant to use our personalities for Him. It is impossible today in a great metropolitan center to build up a parish that you are sure will hold together just as it is after you are gone. In a day of restlessness and insecurity people cling to personalities that interest and inspire them, and this often comes before any loyalty to the institution of the Church which is obviously of greater importance. Robert Norwood told me that when he came down to the United States from Canada, he went to his bishop to talk things over. "I am not sure," he confessed to his Lordship, "whether I have made Christians or Norwoodites." And the wise bishop said, "Probably both—that seems to be the way God works."

And to wind up these problems, how shall we get people reconciled who are at odds or estranged? A man and wife come in who are not getting along. They come with a hope that the Church can help them before it is too late, perhaps with a secret misgiving that it is already too late. Create an atmosphere of ease and leisure. Smile at them, and then perhaps say, "Well, tell me all about it. Maybe I can't help, but I'd like to. Who'll begin?" Draw them out one at a time. Get each to say all that he or she feels. Interpose no contradiction, set forth no premature solution. Let it all come out, unhindered. Give no sign of surprise nor any other emotion, except interest, good nature and faith. As they talk, the real situation will appear to you, where right is, and where wrong is. Don't let your sympathies allow you to "take sides"—the only "side" you want to take is God's side and the right, the only thing you want to be "against" is the sin and wrong in each of them. For the moment, you definitely represent God: they must find in you patience, understanding, justice, compassion, capacity to see the truth and courage to say it, let the chips fall where they may. Only the truth will "make them free." You want them to find in God, for Whom you are standing, a new kind of common ground, a *tertium quid* that is larger than either viewpoint or interest. Now these persons are like dots at the end of a line; you want them to become like base angles of a triangle, with God at the apex. There is healing in the truth, as it comes out, as some of it appears in all its triviality, and as the real difficulty is aired. Many persons are immature in their emotional relationships—and all relationships are primarily emotional. They will get nowhere by going on pointing out each other's faults; they may begin to get somewhere by facing their own. Get them turned in on themselves, not out on one another. "Where do you feel you have been wrong in all this?" The scene changes from accusation to confession—and when it does there may be a miracle on the way. It may take time, for each may be convinced it is entirely the other's fault. Keep praying. Then maybe say, "Remembering your own mistakes and sins in all this, would you be willing to forgive the other person, and to accept forgiveness if it were offered?" You cannot say this before the whole thing is out in the open, the facts, the hurt, the smarting injustice, the real resentment and hate if they be there. But then you can. It is time now (but not earlier) for the suggestion of prayer—maybe in silence on your knees for a time, letting the Spirit convict, letting Christ come with healing forgiveness. If it is not too far for them, get them to put their penitence in a spoken prayer—if too far, then say it for them, putting yourself literally alongside them as identified with their problem and need. This makes a new start. But the same problems will emerge and divide them unless you give them a new basis for living together, including regular devotional habits, private and together, the Church as the place where this "new way" is constantly held up, study and reading to fortify it, and growing application of this personal discovery to other relationships and realms of life. Get them into the stream of God's will and God's grace, till they ask Him to use them to help reconcile others. They will not keep this unless they give it away. That is a spiritual law—for them and for us.

CHAPTER SEVEN

The Church and Evangelism

ANY honest man, looking at our world today, will recognize that of all our manifold needs, the spiritual need is paramount. Everything revolves around two foci: the world of social and political arrangements, and the world of the human soul. We must seek to order our society in ways that are righteous and just, so that there may be increasing brotherhood and peace. But such a world can only be made out of better men and women. Dr. Reinhold Niebuhr says, "The history of mankind exhibits no more ironic experience than the contrast between the sanguine hopes of recent centuries and the bitter experiences of contemporary man." [1] To whatever demonic forces in the universe beyond man's control we may attribute this awful difference between our hopes and our realizations, some of it surely must be attributed to the peculiarly vain hope of modern man that he can re-order his society without at the same time changing his own life. Because this is true, as well as because of

[1] *Faith and History*, p. 1.

the contingencies and mysteriousness of human life, there will always be the need for religion.

The revelations about God, and the insights into man, of the Christian faith are so different from and superior to those of every other "high" religion that it is as if everything else were religions and Christianity itself were Religion. Someone in India, a professor of comparative religion I think it was, asked the great Indian Christian, the Sadhu Sundar Singh, what he saw in Christianity which he had not found in the other religions of India; and the Sadhu said, "Jesus Christ." He is the unique manifestation of God, and it is the unique function of the Church to "know Him and make Him known," to win people to Him and then establish them in Him. Because of the inroads made into modern thought by secularism, humanism, materialism and paganism, we know that the world's mission fields are not the nations and races and islands beyond the seas: America itself is a vast mission field. So is Britain, so are many lands which have known a Christian culture, but have lost the groundwork of that culture which is Christian belief.

All this means that, while the churches have the perennial task of nurturing and training those who are brought within the orbit of Christ, its first task is to bring them within that orbit. Its first task is evangelism. By and large the churches have thought they could do this by three means: a more intellectual approach, better church institutions, and doggedly going ahead with what they were already doing. All power and honour to these three necessary factors. We need, and we have, men quite intellectually capable of handling themselves in the contemporary world; men who can commend the gospel to the human mind, and make it reasonable to believe in it. We need the maintenance of most of our existing church institutions. And we need to keep up our services, our activities, our missionary concern. But everybody knows that these things are simply not enough. People may and often do come within range of these things, only to be disappointed because they miss the characteristic note of Christian power, joy and victory. It all seems like a great, well-run business. The thing the churches ought to be doing is touching everything that they do with the spirit and fire of evangelism. Our own people need awakening, in many instances, quite as much as those outside the Church. How many people have you in your parish who can give a simple, effective, relevant Christian witness, either to an individual, or to a group, such that it will beget faith in Jesus Christ in its hearers? It will be a too small handful in any parish that I know, including my own.

Now there is, of course, a wrong kind of evangelism, and it is not surprising if some clergy are afraid of this and look a little critically upon all kinds of evangelism for this reason. We know that we cannot reach the persons who need the Gospel most, and whom the Church needs most, by tub-thumping, emotional appeals. Some clergy have never seen a kind of evangelism that gives them complete satisfaction. I am sure that some of them would have been extremely uncomfortable at Pentecost, and thought the whole thing much too emotional. The plain fact is that our fairly scholarly sermons, and our reasonably well-run churches, do not often enough either attract or convert people. We desperately need evangelism, and in our souls we know it. We know that of all wrong kinds of evangelism, probably the worst is none at all. It is told that someone said to Dr. Spurgeon that they did not like the way he tried to convert people; and he replied, "I don't altogether like it myself; but I like the way I do it better than the way you don't do it."

The place where evangelism ought to be going on continuously is not in special tents and halls, but in our parish churches. The men who ought to be doing evangelistic work are not experts and specialists, but our ordained clergy of every Church. The time when evangelism ought to be practiced is not a special season, though such periods may have their place, but all the time. It says in Acts 2:47, "And the Lord added to the church daily such as should be saved." That is the everlasting picture of the true Church.

But how shall it come? In my lifetime I have seen whole denominations and highly organized interdenominational movements set about to create an awakening. Where are they now? Except for what the Presbyterians seem to be doing, I do not know of any sustained evangelism of the kind that I believe is going to touch and win and convert many in this generation. Most of it is too highly organized, without being organic. And yet we must not give up. In the report of Section II, on "The Witness of The Church to God's Design," which was received by the World Council of Churches at Amsterdam in 1948, was this paragraph: "It is not within the power of men alone to create a new evangelistic movement. But the Holy Spirit is at work. In the past He has from time to time quickened the Church with power from on high. It is our earnest hope and prayer that He will do a mighty work in our day, giving the Church again wisdom and power rightly to proclaim the good news of Jesus Christ to men. . . . Now, not tomorrow, is the time to act. God does not wait for us to be perfect; He is willing to use very imperfect instruments. What matters is that the instruments should be available for His use. The results of our efforts are not in our hands but His. . . ."

We need a philosophy and a method of evangelism. They cannot be separated. We must have "the Word" and we must have "the Word made flesh." Let me suggest six steps in evangelism:

1. *Exposure.* When the first disciples came in touch with Jesus, they saw and heard and learned things they had never seen nor heard nor learned before. He healed sick people, He changed bad ones into good ones, His life was one long, redeeming action. His words interpreted His deeds. He died on the Cross, having indicated to them very simply the night before the meaning of His death. Then He rose again from the dead. These, too, were part of His "mighty acts." The climate of the New Testament is a climate of action. People were convinced and converted as they came within the stream of that divine action.

This has never stopped. The Church is that company of people amongst whom and through whom Jesus Christ goes on performing the same kind of acts as He performed when He was here. The Church is the normal channel for that stream of power, pouring out from the heart of God to needy men, which is called Christianity. If mighty acts of healing and conversion and spiritual transformation do not take place in any one church, that church has stepped out of the stream and needs to step back into it again. It ought to be possible to come into contact with that stream through a church service. For those far enough along to realize it, probably the surest place to be touched by that stream is the Holy Communion. But many are not so far along. Informal occasions must be found for their inclusion. There is nothing to which the Church needs to turn its attention today more than to the creation of *places of exposure*, where you can take people in order to let them see and feel the work of God's Spirit actively at work in individuals and in companies.

Let me illustrate.

Alcoholics Anonymous is such a place of exposure. More than a hundred thousand men and women in this country alone are "dried up." Why? Because those who are being changed through the truths discovered and made available through that extraordinary movement gather weekly in small companies, where they give testimony and witness to what has happened to them, being alcoholics. When an alcoholic (or for that matter any other human being with a need in his life) listens to what is said, he is powerfully exposed to a faith that can change and save him. These are not lectures, though there is teaching in what they say: they are testimonies, backed by the lives and life story of those who speak. In my opinion, "A.A." has superbly related simple Christian truth to the problem of alcohol. The "open" meetings are places of exposure for those seeking an answer to that need.

Another place of exposure is the gatherings which Ralston Young, Red Cap 42, holds three days a week, Mondays, Wednesdays and Fridays, at noon in an empty car on Track 13 of Grand Central Station. Some years ago Ralston Young was brought back to Christ through the preaching and personal work of a minister whose parish moves on evangelistic lines. He wanted to go to work for Christ. For eight hours a day he was carrying people's bags. He began, as he says, carrying their burdens, too. He would fall into friendly conversation with his patrons, watch and pray for spiritual opportunities, and tell them about Jesus and what had happened in his own life. He made many friends in the Grand Central neighbourhood, and it seemed right for him to begin a meeting for them. Here, in an unlighted and unheated car, you will find a little company of men three times a week. People have been transformed through that little continuing place of exposure. It takes one converted man, and then another, till you have a nucleus. Every church should have groups of people like this, meeting in homes, offices and other places of the city. Some will come to them who will not come to a formal church service—yet. Think about it—is there anywhere in your parish or neighbourhood such a company that through prayer, related Bible study, mutual exchange, and speaking out of their hearts, affords a place of exposure to a person curious or eager for a discovery of Christ?

2. *Explanation.* When people were exposed to Christ through what He had done, they began asking questions: "Who . . . what . . . how?" I heard a scholarly man say recently that he thought most of Jesus' teaching was given as explanation and justification of His action. He did something, it provoked questions, His teaching was the answer. He did not come down out of a mountain, speak and then retire again. He went apart and found power, came back to the haunts of men, met their needs of body, mind and soul, and then taught *in the presence of the power of these deeds.* The kind of questions you ask in the presence of spiritual power, and the kind of questions you ask after a religious lecture, are entirely different: the first is a life question, the second may be only a brain question.

Preaching is, of course, meant to be explanation like that, and at its best it is. It should come out of a man who is close to God and close to life, but also close to frequent incursions of God into life. Its real matter is not ideas, but events: what God has done in history in Christ, and all this brought up to date and close to home through daily discoveries of this power on the part of present-day people. The trouble with so much preaching is that it is *explanation apart from event.* Nothing much is really going on spiritually, in the preacher's own life, or the life of those to whom he ministers: so he goes to books for his inspiration. That is what makes preaching dry. It may be true, but it is abstract. Religion so easily degenerates into theory. The imagination must be caught before the mind will ask life questions, or really face the challenge of Christ. How often do we preach emptily and to no avail, because our lives are not sufficiently immersed in continuous prayer and ever-fresh discovery of God's grace working in and through contemporary people, including ourselves!

Sometimes explanation is best given privately in interviews. A person goes to a place of exposure, sees something potent and real, and wants to know more about it. What is said in the meeting may help answer his questions, but he may need to get alone with a

Christian that knows "the way," and have an interview. His questions may be all tied up with personal problems that can only be faced with one person. Some questions can only be answered as people are willing to take moral and spiritual steps first. "He that willeth to do His will shall know . . ." We must help them face the question: "Am I willing to do His will in all things?" For that may be the pre-condition to finding an answer to the question. A young man I know is perplexed about whether he stays in business or goes into the ministry: I asked him if he were praying about it, and he said, "Yes, some. I guess I am afraid of what He might tell me if I really prayed about it." He can't get the answer to the question till he is ready to surrender himself to God. When he wills to do His will, he will know.

3. *Experiment.* After seeing what Christianity does, and hearing what it is, the next step is to try to put it to work in your own life. For in all life, and especially in the Christian life, we learn by doing. People associated themselves with the apostles and disciples, till the things that those men and women experienced began happening to them. Everybody can go where Christ is believed in and worshiped, and let themselves become increasingly part of that believing, worshiping company. Everybody can begin to pray. Everybody

can read the kind of books that induce spiritual belief and discovery. Everybody can try being more loving towards others, more generous in judgments, more filled with prayer for every human contact.

There is a characteristic Christian way of being changed—a Christian psychology as well as a Christian philosophy. I think it goes something like this. When we come in contact anywhere with Christ, at work in others, or directly, we feel both elated and disturbed—elated because nothing in the world so fills us with hope and joy as the vision of true spiritual power and reality—disturbed because we are so far from Him in our hearts and know what a struggle may lie before us to give Him right of way in our own lives. This place of our need is the place of His entrance. Someone said truly that we take hold of Christ by the handle of our sins. The facing of ourselves as we really are in God's sight, the admission of our sins to ourselves and possibly to another trained Christian, the digging out of the fearsome and shameful and black defeats that hold us down, is the only condition of being changed. Then we bring these things to Christ, and ask for His forgiveness. How intuitively real does the Cross become to people who really recognize their sins and their own powerlessness to do anything about them! How real is that self-surrender which does not cry out in general, "O Lord, take my life," but instead says, "Lord, I give to thee now my lust, and my fear, and my selfishness, and my pride. I took that money and will repay it. I stole that reputation and will try to make restitution. And with these sins, I would surrender myself altogether." After this, prayer becomes a reality. The Bible is the food on which converted lives feed. The Church becomes their company, their family. The Holy Communion is the ever-present, helping "Hand of Grace" reached down to them. It is, I believe, entirely right that all of us should approach these ancient "means of grace" in an experimental frame of mind—how can we do other, until they themselves have convinced us of their efficacy?—remembering only that we do not so much put them on trial as to their efficacy, as they put us on trial about the sincerity and sustained nature of our experiment.

All Christian people ought to know how to make the Christian experiment, and how to help others to make it. It is as definite as my taking my study lamp and plugging its wire into the outlet in the floor board and turning on the light. God is like the vast, unseen Dynamo. Christ and His Church are like the outlets into the present world, where the power of the dynamo becomes available. Self-surrender is the act of "plugging in" to the divine current. And prayer is like turning on the light of inspiration. Obviously the experiment is not so mechanical as this, but it is just as definite. It is not a complicated thing to try the Christian experiment. One has seen too many people do it, and seen the results follow.

4. *Experience.* What an astonishing experience for a first-century Jew or pagan, coming from such different backgrounds, to find the utter reality of Christ, His response to their act of faith, His answers to their prayers, His living Presence there *for them* in the Eucharist! And then those changes in personality, in outlook, in values, in habits, in the very chemistry of the body itself, which "confirm the word with signs following"! It is still so. When one honestly makes the experiment, there comes to him such a harmony and unity in his own spirit, such a rightness in his relationships, such a sense of the utter reality of God and of His touch upon us and the privilege of cooperating with Him, as leaves no room for question.

It is important for us to put Christian experience in its rightful setting. It does not come first, and is not in itself the final proof of the truth of Christianity. We must remember Jonathan Edwards' warning, "They put their experiences in the place of Christ . . . they take more comfort in their discoveries than in Christ discovered." There is always a danger of that. Christians do not try to finagle what they want from God: we do not stand off and say that Christian experience makes for happiness, therefore give us Christian experience. And yet, how barren and dry would be the religious life without the merciful dealings of God in which He allows us to realize the benefits of His love and grace in experience that lifts us above the common pressures of life! A wise friend of mine, Starr Daily, says that the cults emphasize the gifts without the Giver, and the orthodox Church emphasizes the Giver without the gifts: and what we need is to emphasize *both*–Christ in all the full panoply of His power, in all the rich setting of the historic faith held and practiced in the organic Church, and then also the gifts and experiences, the assurances through events that He alone could have caused, when we are in vital league with Him! Christ and true faith in Him are more important than any experience which He may give us. But some people find the experience first and work back through it to the faith, e.g. the blind man who could not tell much of who Christ was, but could say with assurance after he was healed, "Whereas I was blind, now I see."

5. *Expression.* Having heard the Gospel, having tried faith and the way of faith, and become assured

that it is "the way," then people must begin to express it in their daily lives because it is true.

We must do what God did, wrap our Gospel not in words only but in life. Sometimes it seems as if God said all He could say in words through the prophets and the Old Testament; and then decided to put it all into One Life where the simplest and wisest both might read it. "The Word was made flesh, and dwelt among us. . . ." There must be our own little incarnations of faith in life.

A Christian life of integrity and unselfishness, indeed even one unexpected act of unselfishness, is a great witness for Christ. When you see a person living outside himself, living for other people, ready to sacrifice himself for them or to lose himself in a great cause, you know that there is a Power in his life that is not common. It was said of William Borden, who gave his privileged young life to serve the unprivileged in Egypt, and died there soon after his graduation from Yale (and the words are graven on his tombstone in Cairo), "Apart from Christ there is no explanation of such a life."

But example is only an opener. None of us can by our example alone give witness to all the rich fullness of the Christian faith, in the Holy Trinity, in Christ as God, as Atoner for the sins of the world, as Lord of life and death through the Resurrection. Our moral examples are the merest and most inadequate footnote to this. Only faith itself can leap up to these eternal verities, and declare them in words. We can only indicate these things by our worship, our adoration and our witness to Him.

We cannot witness in a vacuum: we must first know the people to whom we witness, discover what they are like, what their needs are. Some of us try to bring our answers too fast, before we have got people to ask the questions they answer. Religious arguments between two minds do often more harm than good; but understanding, sympathy, humility are the vehicles for the simple affirmation of our own faith and its relation to the needs of others. Recently a young man has been attending some "cells" where the kind of thing discussed in this book has been the essence of what was said and done: it went right to his heart, and within the first four weeks he has talked with six of his friends. He says, "It all comes about quite naturally if you are vitally interested yourself." Witness is the joyous overflow of a person who is so enthusiastic about what Christ is doing for him that he just cannot keep quiet. It presupposes a faith and an experience. There needs to be humour in it, and naturalness, and it should deal with real problems in real life and Christ's power to meet and solve them.

This expression will show itself in one's daily place of business in a new attitude of mind on the part of anyone who has found Christ. When tension goes out of our lives, it goes out of our relationships, and those about us feel it. Business men drop off with heart attacks at fifty and sixty because they know no way to reduce the tensions and pressures under which they live. These tensions communicate themselves to others in the office, the home, the farm, the factory. And when faith comes in, they tend to disappear. New kinds of relationships spring up with old acquaintances. We stop using people and begin caring about them. One of them notices a change and remarks on it, and this leads to a talk, perhaps to the beginning of a weekly gathering, before work begins in the morning, or at the lunch hour. Others hear of it and are invited in. And this may be the slow-working but real leaven that changes the spirit of an industry. If fellowship is there first, many things may follow in the direction of greater sharing in the planning and profits of the business. Where nations or businesses or individuals are only interested in keeping what they have, and not in a steady advance towards more justice and fairness, more advantages and opportunities, they are bound to suffer for it in the end. As nature abhors a vacuum, history seems to abhor stagnation. If we had steady, evolutionary Christian development, and this were as much the passion of labor and management as money is, we should have no fear of the revolutionary Communist development which may, nevertheless, be God's instrument of judgment upon a society too content with leaving things exactly as they are. But there is a world of difference between Christians voluntarily sharing the goods of life, and Communists seeking to take what belongs to others.

6. *Expectation.* This is not so much a step in a process as the climate in which the process should be carried out. Jesus said, "According to thy faith be it done unto thee." If you hope little, you get little: if you believe much, much happens. Faith is very near to imagination, and imagination is a capacity to see things as they are not but might be. One of the most pitiful things about some churches and some Christians is their low level of expectation. They go to church, read their Bibles, even say their prayers, with no expectation of anything happening, and–according to their faith it is done unto them: nothing *does* happen.

We must expect more of God. It seems as if our faith is an invisible wire along which His power is transmitted to us and to others. Little wires cannot take big charges; big wires are needed. Only great faith releases God's great power. But great faith simply means great surrender, putting ourselves more deeply at His command, so that if He wills it He may partly answer our prayers through ourselves.

We must expect more of ourselves. Too many Christians, too many clergy, are content with an uncreative routine of life. It has been too long since they saw or were part of a miracle. We need to let the Spirit fire us with the love of God, with love for people. We need to think of ourselves as His agents and channels, able to transmit His power to other people, according to their need. We must never say that we could not be part of a spiritual awakening or have a share in it. Let it start in us, and we cannot help being part of it!

And we must expect more of others. Those lackluster folk in the pews can glow and shine with a radiant and contagious faith. Those pagans you cannot seem to touch will respond when you love them, serve them and pray for them. Your brother clergy, about whom you are perhaps often critical, are hungry for the same spiritual reality as you long for yourself, and will respond to it when you mediate it through caring and humility and generous concern. Begin praying for new relations with your own family, with your trustees, with your people, with your neighbors. Let God make a new person out of you, and they will see it and respond. It is often we ourselves who block the awakening we pray for: we must change, and then we may be used to bring it about.

A changed Church can change the world. We ministers do more than any others to make the Church what it is, so it will take changed ministers to change the Church. The task before us is beyond any human capacity to meet. But with God, all things are possible. He can, if we will.

Date Due

Thesis			
MAY 28 '65			
1-5-67			
1-19-67			
OCT 15 '[illegible]			
MAY 13 '76			
DEC 1 '76			
DEC 15 '76			
12/17/80			